More Literary Houses

More Literary Houses

by
Rosalind Ashe

Facts On File Publications
460 Park Avenue South
New York, N.Y. 10016

Design and Art Direction by Steve Henderson
Plans and sketches by David Heal
Researched by Imogen Taylor

Library of Congress Cataloguing in Publication Data

Ashe, Rosalind.
  More literary houses.

  1. Architecture, Domestic, in literature.
2. Dwellings in literature. 3. Setting (Literature).
I. Title.
PN56.A73A83 1983   823'.009'22   83-5565
ISBN 0-87196-422-8

Printed in Singapore

987654321

Foreword

It's been said that reading a great novel is the nearest mortals can get to perfect freedom; that no other pursuit, and certainly no other art, allows us such all-knowing, all-seeing power: we can indeed float free, swimming godlike through the minds, the hearts, of emperors and schoolboys, kings and kitchenmaids. Even the most "in depth" documentary keeps us earthbound with fact and weighty judgement; biography and autobiography have their own clearly defined limits. But the novelist is at liberty to use as much of history and reality as is needed to build the structure of his choice, like a bird making its nest with twigs, bedstraw, human hair, scraps of velvet, and lining it with any stolen jewels and trinkets that catch his magpie's eye.

Such fiction is perhaps closest to poetry in its breadth of choice, its range of sympathy: it too can see the world in Blake's grain of sand or in Milton's lost Paradise. But with a great novel the peculiar compression and swiftness of the poet's view is expanded: no longer contained by that wrought-iron grille of lines, it stretches out in time and space, creating a room, a dwelling, a little world to move about in, between its front and back covers.

Pictures, on the other hand, define: that is their power and charm; perhaps their danger – they draw a line round a point of view. But they have the unique ability to freeze and perpetuate the passing moment; they go a long way toward satisfying another need in mortals: to hold onto an experience, thus outwitting Time itself.

The attraction, therefore, of an illustrated novel is the freedom to roam, with maps and images to suggest our route, or show us where we have been. As before in *Literary Houses*, the artists and author can only give their own views, which others may use for comparison, like travellers' tales, or simply as a gateway into these great books – some of them quite forbiddingly large. The chief difficulty in writing these "introductory" pieces lay, therefore, in attempting to give some small notion of such superlative master-works; and, although I knew most of them, re-reading them first made me feel my task

was hopeless, swiftly followed by an overwhelming desire to share them as best I could: if only by saying, "It goes something like this..." as one might hum a tune to recall a great symphony. But I have left it to the artists to show the structure and the key changes, so to speak: description is their field; while I have tried simply to catch the flavour of the work, the feeling of the places, the plot, the characters.

As before, we have chosen books in which the houses are very much part of the story. If there was a unifying theme in the first collection, it was the sense of mystery in all of them – and almost inevitably, therefore, a strong flavour of the "gothic". This time we explore houses in France, Germany, Italy, Russia, Kafka's Mittel-Europe, Sicily, Jamaica, England and America. The houses range from the O'Haras' gracious mansion in the warm South of *Gone With The Wind*, to the Rostovs' snow-trimmed Moscow house, and their country estate, in *War And Peace*; from Kafka's *Castle* to P. G. Wodehouse's Castle Blandings. There is the solid burghers' status symbol of the Buddenbrooks, set in the merchant town of Lübeck, the connoisseur's Florentine villa in Henry James's *Portrait of a Lady*, and the careless grandeur of the Leopard Prince's country Palace. In *Middlemarch*, we have the contrast between a manor and a town house, the dwellings of the two very different women who dominate George Eliot's masterpiece; and finally two enchanting, decaying buildings: the childhood home in Jamaica of Mr Rochester's strange bride, and the lost domain of another's childhood: *Le Grand Meaulnes* himself – his for one magical winter's day, never to be seen again.

In finding a way into each different world, I have chosen a voice, either from among the characters themselves, or of someone who wanders into the story; and if there is a unifying theme in this book, it is Variety. For our intention was to range further afield, confront the giants of fiction on their mountain tops – and hopefully bring back something to keep. Something to remind us of the Realms of Gold; like that schoolboy with his silken waistcoat, the only proof of his Lost Domain.

Contents

MARGARET MITCHELL

(1900 – 1949)

Margaret Mitchell was born in Atlanta, Georgia, the daughter of a lawyer. She was a shy but observant child, her mother never allowing her reticence to detract from a duty to courtesy, a trait common in the "gentle southerners" of the United States. She had a contented and secure family life, often spending her summer months on a farm owned by two spinster aunts. It was here that she was encouraged to take part in the family evening prayers, to attend lively parties and to listen attentively to the tales of old retainers and their memories of the Civil War. An interest in family and social history was inspired by her father and at school Margaret Mitchell began to write short stories, much enjoyed by hordes of admirers who relished her good looks and sharp wit. In 1918 she enrolled at Smith College in Massachussets but returned home a year later following the death of her mother. She took on the care of her father and at the same time joined the staff of the *Atlanta Journal Sunday Magazine*.

After a brief and disastrous first marriage, Margaret Mitchell married for a second time, to John Marsh, and dedicated herself to home life. Her husband suggested she continue to write, and having perused the Atlanta library's stock of history books, she began her novel, *Gone With the Wind*. The work took ten years to complete, the pile of manuscript ever increasing but hidden away from interested eyes until 1935, when she was persuaded to show it to a representative of the Macmillan Company. Thrilled at his find, the publisher hurried the book onto the market where it was an instant success. The author was inundated by streams of callers, Scarlett O'Hara look-alikes and essays on character analysis. Preferring to shun such publicity, Margaret Mitchell stayed quietly in Atlanta and in 1937 was awarded the Pulitzer Prize. The novel was made into a spectacularly successful film in 1939 by David O. Selznick.

Though she wrote many short stories, *Gone With the Wind* was Margaret Mitchell's only novel. She died in Atlanta following a motor accident at the age of 49.

Chapter 1

GONE WITH THE WIND

"He had a picture painted of the house just after it was built: a typical gracious Southern home – not as grand as the Wilkes's Twelve Oaks – of whitewashed brick with a shingle roof; a pair of classic columns and a verandah where chairs were set out in the evening. O'Hara used to claim it was built according to no architectural plan whatever: he'd added extra rooms where and when it pleased him."

R. Ashe

Thanks – don't mind if I do. Wine, as a matter of fact— Well I declare: that's real handsome! *Sure* we can handle a bottle... Pardon me? Oh, that red French stuff I usually have, Harry... So – you new around these parts?

Hey now, wait a minute. How'd you know my name, mister? No, I'm not running from anything – memories, maybe, like most folk – But hell, strangers can't just walk up to you and start in— That lady I was with? Why, "we're just good friends" I think is the answer to that. And what's that to you, might I enquire? Landsakes, you sure have some nerve – OK: So you've had a few before this – but that doesn't give you the right to—

She reminds you of Scarlett. A bit. You've met up with Scarlett then. Well well: so, and who's she married to nowadays? Oh you poor boy! You know, I *reckoned* you looked like you were sickening for something bad. Gotten the old bug good and proper, eh? Have another glass: come on – you paid for it.

Now let me get this right. Katy Scarlett O'Hara Hamilton Kennedy Butler told you she was a – a "bad risk"? But you still want to marry her. Might I ask, have you the necessary capital for this venture? I see. And still she turned you down. Scarlett must have changed some. I still don't see just why she sent you to me, friend. OK, I may be the one who knows her best: "the only man who ever understood me" – that's what she said? And *you* think she's still in love with me? For want of a better word...

Well, I'm not standing in anyone's way, Mister— Mister? – Bouverie: not yours nor any other sucker's. Sure I'm bitter: her timing was always lousy...like the occasion on our honeymoon when she started crying in her sleep and I hugged her up – I thought it was the old recurring nightmare, you know? Or maybe you don't ... little girl lost in the fog – and she said "Oh Ashley!"... Sorry, friend – just thinking out loud.

Oh sure I can tell you about her. I met the O'Haras long ago, before the wind of war. The Golden Age, my friend, that you're too young to recall. You're a Yankee anyway – right? – for all the fancy French name – no offence, Mister. Harry! This bottle's mine, OK? On the slate. But you couldn't even imagine that world-in-the-evening – as I saw it to be even then; though the fine Southern beaux and belles didn't

Preceding pages: *Tara, Gerald O'Hara's southern mansion, from a painting he'd commissioned shortly after it was built.*

know what time it was – 'cepting Barbecue time or Fish-fry time or Horse-race time or Dancin' time. And it was always Flirtin' time... She was a heller: and I could see it right away in the middle of that great high-falutin barbecue party of the Wilkes's. She was tormenting all the young men, the Tarleton twins and poor young Charles Hamilton – though he was good as promised to Honey Wilkes.

Sure, I picked her out right off – not just because of the beaux buzzing round her, but— Well, there was a *spirit* in her, a deep and devilish charm: something wild and strong like it's never been tamed nor beaten, and never would be, I felt. Oh she was pretty all right, but by no means perfect in her features— But you know her looks, my friend: and she hadn't changed a lot over the years when I said goodbye. Grown something harder with all she's had to go through; but the same spark and flash – the turn of the head – all the same pretty tricks... Deep down? I'm tempted to say, deep down she's profoundly shallow— No: at heart she's just a tough Irish immigrant, quick-tempered and passionate, making her way in the world and using any weapon to hand: looks, guile, and one hell of a will. Just like her father in many ways: the son and heir he never had – never raised: the old man buried three, you know.

But three daughters he kept. Katy Scarlett was the eldest; Careen's in the Convent now; and you didn't get to meet Suellen, I suppose, at the old Tara? Well that figures: she never did forgive Scarlett for stealing Frank Kennedy from under her nose – oh yes indeed: her own sister. But not for her own sake: all for Tara. That place was her real love – maybe her only abiding love; anyway the driving force in her life. And you'd have to accept that, my friend, to even begin to know her. It wasn't just a house and a cotton plantation – it was a passion, a cause. Wonderful country, though: rich red North Georgia earth, fierce sun, deep shade; if you're born in that sort of paradise you never get it out of your blood.

The house itself Gerald O'Hara built not twenty years before the time I met them. He was a self-made man who'd arrived as a blue-eyed Irish thug of twenty-one – and much the same forty years on, a thick-set, bull-necked little tough with County Meath still strong in his mouth. A lucky gambler: that's how he started making his money; and folks used to say he built his great white house then saw he needed a proper Southern Lady to put in it – but they were all amazed when he carried off Ellen Robillard, the toast

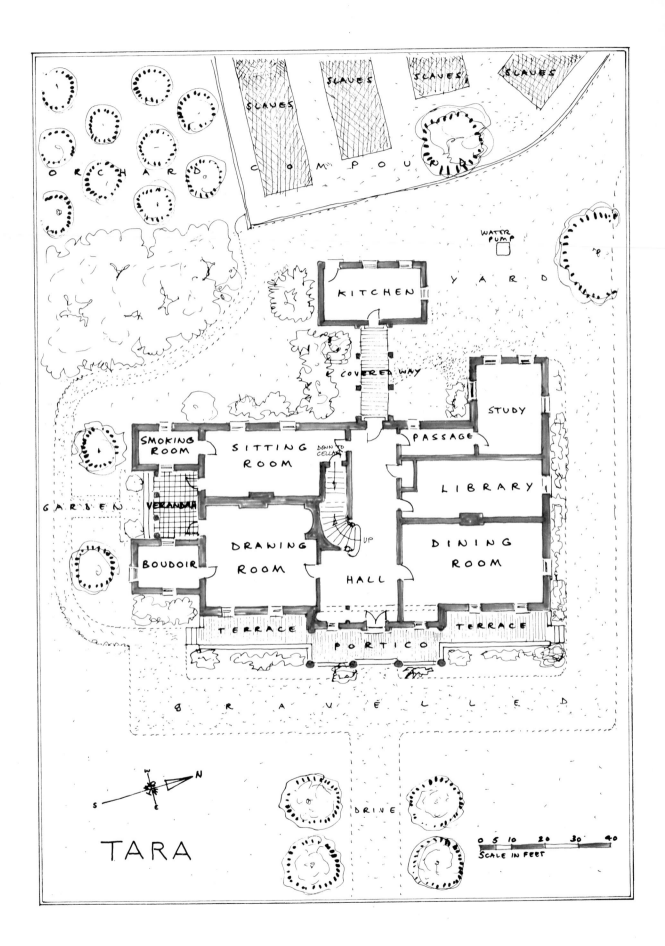

SLAVES SLAVES SLAVES SLAVES

ORCHARD COMPOUND

WATER PUMP

KITCHEN YARD

COVERED WAY

SMOKING ROOM SITTING ROOM DOWN TO CELLAR PASSAGE STUDY

GARDEN VERANDAH LIBRARY

BOUDOIR DRAWING ROOM UP DINING ROOM

HALL

TERRACE PORTICO TERRACE

GRAVELLED

N W E S

DRIVE

0 5 10 20 30 40
SCALE IN FEET

TARA

Above: *Scarlett's bedroom on the morning of that fateful party at Twelve Oaks where Ashley Wilkes announced his engagement to Another. Light and airy, the room had a good view of the drive and anyone who might be coming to visit.*

Left: *Although the house had been built "to no architectural plan", the hall was fine, with a wide curving stair, and you could see through into the back where a covered way led to the servants' quarters.*

of Savannah, with high-and-mighty French blood in her veins... Everyone liked him: and he was so proud of his house, his "real lady" – one of the two sweetest-natured women that walked this earth – and his three lovely daughters. Not that he needed to put on airs by then, for he was quite the country gentleman; the only part he played was the Hard Nut – and fooled no one, even his coloured slaves, who knew just how soft-hearted he was.

He had a picture painted of the house just after it was built: a typical gracious Southern home – not as grand as the Wilkes's Twelve Oaks – of whitewashed brick with a shingle roof; a pair of classic columns and a verandah where chairs were set out in the evening. O'Hara used to claim it was built according to no architectural plan whatever: he'd added extra rooms where and when it pleased him. But the hall was fine, with a wide curving stair right up to the top; and you could see through into the back where a covered way led to the servants' quarters. Scarlett especially loved the dining room: a comfortable, friendly place, where the family would sit on after dinner of an evening, listening to Mamma's gentle gossip or Papa holding forth, while her sisters embroidered or read romantic novels by the light of the big oil lamp. Her own bedroom was right above the dining room, and both had a good view of the cedar drive and anyone who might be coming to visit.

Of course she didn't think of the house as "new": it mellowed over the years – you're right, the war did a mite more than mellowing. But she remembered it with all the wistaria and suchlike hanging in curtains from the balustrade, and the floors between the rag rugs real dark and glossy with the years of polishing. ... I guess her most favourite hideyhole was Ellen

O'Hara's study at the back: the desk where Mamma scratched away with a quill pen at the plantation accounts, and Papa's rocker, and the saggy old sofa no longer smart enough for visitors. She told me that's where she'd run away to and cry her little heart out when her schemes went all wrong...

Like Ashley Wilkes' engagement. Announced officially on that same day I first laid eyes on her – some irony, eh? – at Twelve Oaks: a whole day of barbecue lunch and siesta time and then supper and dancing. I don't reckon she really believed her beloved Ashley would go marry that skinny little mouse Melanie long as Scarlett O'Hara, the Belle of Georgia, was his for the taking. She'd never understood him: I guess that's what kind of fascinated her – who am I to say? Dammit, I really liked the man, though we had little enough in common: he was dreamy and bookish; had "ideals", you know? And he'd done the Grand Tour. Oh, I've been to Paris and London, but not like that: Paris is the place I know for women's fashions, not "the home of the Louvre". Ashley lived in his head; he would never have done for Scarlett. But gentle Miss Melly understood him— That's right: hers was the other sweet nature— Not Scarlett, oh no! though she'd have appeared sweet enough that first day to an unpractised eye; and like I say, these boys were buzzing round her, while Suellen, and India and Honey Wilkes and the rest could only sit by and look daggers. They must have known what was up; even an outsider like me cottoned on to it pretty fast: that she was "just mo'tified" (as she'd say) by Ashley's attentions to Melanie – sure, a dun hedge-sparrow beside that glittering hummingbird, but his choice – and Scarlett was set on being brightest and best to show everyone she didn't give a damn; to show him what he was passing up.

It was like coming in on the middle of a theatrical drama, that barbecue. I wasn't just an outsider, you see: I was a *rank* outsider, with scandals to my name – I'd had to go north for some months to get out. No longer a young buck neither: probably had more to say to the middle-aged landowners than those doomed beaux and their feather-brained sweethearts. So I mostly looked on; and they didn't like it much when I stopped watching and tried to put them straight about the coming war – coming soon; and its very real danger, for all their brave talk and heroic gestures. "The gentlemen versus the rabble", was how they saw it: "It'll be over in a month and we'll have them howling"...

Opposite: *Scarlett returned from Atlanta to find that during the war Tara had been used as a Yankee headquarters. The Northerners had passed through like a swarm of locusts.*

"But what iron foundries have we," I enquired, "south of the Mason-Dixon Line? What cannon factories, iron and coal mines? Warships, perhaps? Not one: they could bottle up our harbours in a week. All we've got, gentlemen, is cotton, slaves and arrogance—" or something along those lines... I think Ashley Wilkes – for all he was one of the first to volunteer – maybe saw something of the true threat; and deaf old Mr Macrae tried to tell them what war was like in terms of hunger and mud and dysentery – but he just shocked the ladies and got hushed up for his pains.

They didn't like my realism no more'n if a critic from the front row had stepped up onto their fancy white-column stage: only their Southern good manners spared me; and I retired to the library – where my siesta was interrupted by Act Two: little Miss Fire-and-Brimstone herself making a mighty powerful bid for her lost love, getting a graceful turn-down, and hurling crockery around as soon as he'd Exited Right. But the fireworks display when I emerged from the depths of the sofa – the Witness of Her Shame, dramatically speaking – was *really* something. I guess I realised way back then she was the right girl for me. Still I was a long way from catching her: she'd married twice and had two kids before I got her.

The first time around, she married for spite, when she saw she couldn't have her precious Ashley. Married within two weeks: every rule and convention about nice girls and long engagements and Hope Chests were swept away you see; for the war had started and the young men were marching off, excited like they might be late for the party... Scarlett was a widow within two months: Charlie Hamilton died of pneumonia, not even a hero – Mo'tifying! When I next saw her it was in Atlanta: an eighteen-year-old widow lumbered with a baby she didn't like; very down-in-the-mouth she was, crow-black crêpe from top to toe, and no question of being free again and having fun. Oh no: confined to good works and a sad demeanour: *that* was still a rule. At least it was better for her to be in Atlanta, even with Melanie and Aunt Pittipat. Stuck at home or with matronly relatives she'd been pining away – but in that brash young

town, and not far from the battle-front itself, everything was happening: soldiers marching through, hospitals being set up, factories – any factory – turning out war goods as best they could; and there was more than enough to keep the worthy womenfolk of the town busy, especially when the wounded started pouring in. Me? No, I hadn't joined up: still wheeling and dealing, running the blockade – not just with supplies but with frocks and furbelows for the ladies.

Then things got pretty rough; and I guess Scarlett's first real appeal to me was when she needed help to get away from the city. Her aunt and most of the gentry had gotten out; but Scarlett was held back when Melanie started having her baby. Lord Almighty, that was a hot day! High summer, and the wooden town burning, and no doctor that wasn't sweating among the wounded and dying. So she found herself playing midwife, provider and protector to the sweet, brave

wife of her precious Ashley Wilkes. Scarlett was a reluctant heroine that day; at least I managed to find her a horse and cart, and got them out of the blazing town and on the road. There I left them; and, inspired by Lord knows what – that reluctant heroine maybe – I joined the losing side, my own dear crazy South.

Well, she may have told you of that terrible journey to get back to Tara, safety and refuge in the arms of her adored mother. Scarlett was homing like a salmon, with all that tireless energy and blind instinct for survival. But the Tara she found when at last she got them there was not quite what she had held in her mind's eye over those weary miles.

It had been used as a Yankee headquarters; and so, though the building itself was standing, the house and gardens and stores had been ransacked; silver, crockery, pictures, livestock: pretty well everything had been taken; and her mother was dead. She found her father turned senile by disasters, her sisters sick,

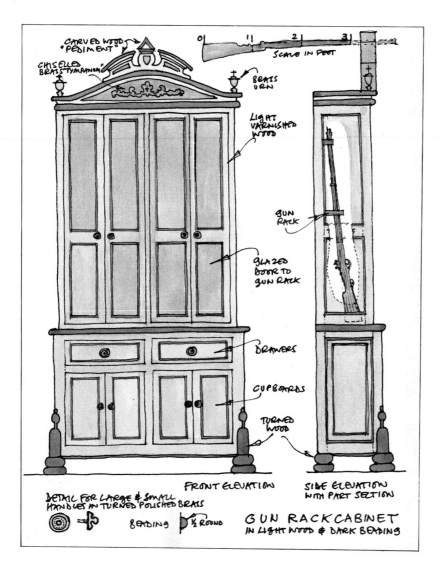

Left: *Before the war a gun rack stood in the hall, filled with Gerald O'Hara's favourite firearms.*

and only three servants on the place: the faithful Mammy, Pork the butler and his wife Dilcey. And to this household she brought the ill and exhausted Melly, the newborn baby, her own little son, and Prissy, her useless maid and not much more than a picaninny herself. Some homecoming.

So: she'd been through danger and hardships, seen death, and history in the making, fought her way home – and that's when the tough times *really* start. You get to thinking you're so low you can't go no further – but oh, indeed you can. And you have to fight to keep your folks alive – if only as the labourers of the future. Anyone fit to walk you get out in the fields to dig and plant, or hunt for food. You fight their weariness and your own every hour of every day... Not the sort of life that comes natural for a southern belle. History does not relate just what she told old Pork when he said, "But Miss Scarlett, us can't do no field-hand business; Ah's allus bin a house nigger—"!

So – pretty kitten grew up into mother tiger: guarding, hunting, even killing to protect herself and her brood and her territory. Later when peace came, and she'd almost got the old place on its feet again,

Above: *Ellen O'Hara's study at the back of the house, where she dealt with the plantation accounts, was the real family room. With its saggy old sofa and air of comfort it was Scarlett's favourite place to hide.*

with more helpers now – yes, even the long-lost Ashley home from the wars – she did what some say was worse 'n killing. You see, she had to get money for the new taxes, and, rather than lose Tara, she cheated and lied her way into marrying her sister's old beau. And not before she'd tried it out on me. No, she wouldn't have told you of that, but you said you wanted to know what she was like deep down. Friend, she dolled herself up as fine as she could, and she came and offered me anything – everything – if I'd come across with the three hundred dollars to pay those taxes... Reckon I'm only telling you 'cause you asked; as things were, I was in no position to take her up on it: I was a prisoner, and waiting to be shot. Well, she went off without a backward glance and found Frank Kennedy building his big new store. And so Tara was saved...

But you saw the new Tara: the one *I* built for her. Mighty fancy, don't you think? With all its turrets and

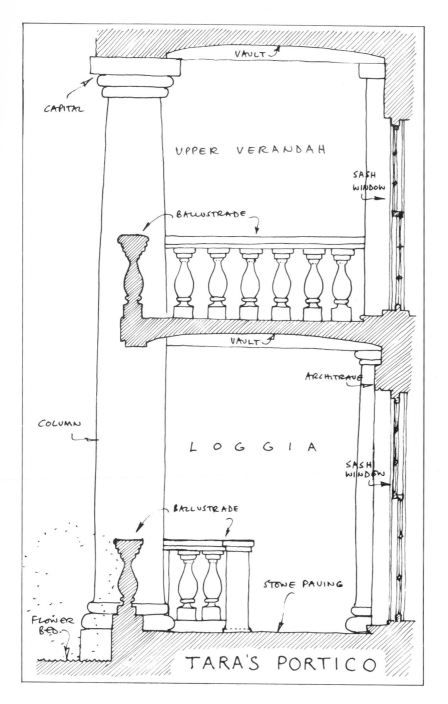

CAPITAL

VAULT

UPPER VERANDAH

SASH
WINDOW

BALLUSTRADE

VAULT

ARCHITRAVE

COLUMN

L O G G I A

SASH
WINDOW

BALLUSTRADE

STONE PAVING

FLOWER
BED

TARA'S PORTICO

balconies. I offered her something along the lines of the old house; but no, it had to be the latest new-fangled thing and even bigger: if she couldn't make the society ladies approve of her, by God she'd impress them – they mightn't like her but she'd make damn sure they envied her. She had a good head for money: when poor Frank was conveniently killed (he'd been involved in the start of the Klu Klux Klan, as they all were; and he died defending his women-folk), then Scarlett had sole control of the business and ran it quite unscrupulously, making money but not friends.

Know something? I reckon "liking" that girl was hard, but falling in love with her was all too easy: not just the crowds of handsome young cannon-fodder in those early days, but grown men like Frank Kennedy and me. Even Ashley – oh yes, he was infatuated alright, mesmerised – but strong enough to break away. And now you. And the good Lord alone knows how many other fools as well. But there were maybe only three or four that were deep-down fond of her: her father, her mother, little Melly – against all the odds – and Mammy. Oh no: I was nevery really *fond* of Scarlett. Old Mammy, now: she could see clear through all those pretty ways, same as I could: she raised her and chided her and berated her and was outraged at her downright wickedess – and still loved her. Yes, old Mammy stayed the course all right. Not me.

And Scarlett? Well, she loved Tara, her parents, and Mammy. And Ashley: always. No, not her children; not really. Bonny maybe, her third: *our* child. If Bonny had lived I guess we might still be rubbing along. As for loving me – I rate that as another of her pretty whims, now. She may think she

Following pages: After the Yankees moved on it was Scarlett who ran Tara, digging and planting, struggling for existence. They had taken everything but her will to survive – and the family silver, hidden in the well.

did: I was useful; and I whirled her about, gave her a good time. What's more, she needed a rich husband: she was just old enough and almost wise enough to begin to want some respect from society... Oh, she'll install you all right, never fear: she's clawed her way up to the top of the heap and now, I guess, she needs a fine gentleman for her fine new house.

My plans? My immediate plan, dear sir, here and now, is to top off the French red with a good shot of Southern Comfort...

HENRY JAMES

(1843 – 1916)

Born on Manhattan Island, New York, Henry James spent much of his childhood travelling in Europe with his family. One of four children, all very talented, James was a quiet child, deeply interest in the arts.

After reading Law at Harvard University, he submitted some literary criticism to the *North American Review*, while writing passages and stories at the same time. *The Portrait of A Lady* was published in 1881, closely followed by *The Bostonians* and *The Princess Casamassima*, both written in London.

Following the death of his father, brother and sister, James returned to the United States, then travelled to Europe once more, staying for some time in Venice and Florence. A love for England persuaded him to go back there and he eventually became a British subject and bought a house in Rye, Sussex, where he spent much time writing. At the outbreak of the War, he assisted the Allied war effort by visiting hospitals, by that time being a considerable celebrity. He was awarded the Order of Merit by King George V on New Year's Day 1916 and died in London on 28 February of that year.

Chapter 2

THE PORTRAIT OF A LADY

"Isabel went with her friend through a wide, high court, where a clear shadow rested below and a pair of light-arched galleries, facing each other above, caught the upper sunshine upon their slim columns and the flowering plants in which they were dressed. There was something grave and strong in the place; it looked somehow as if, once you were in, you would need an act of energy to get out."

But why *him*? That's what I could not make out. Isabel Archer was young and beautiful and suddenly very rich: she could have married anyone... Well, now that I've seen it, I do absolutely insist the place had something to do with it – yes, that villa of his outside Florence, you know: his hilltop lair that he made so much of withdrawing to, and leaving the world behind.

Not that it was completely "my cup of tea" as they say in Britain; but I could see right away what must have appealed to my wide-eyed, romantic, highminded friend. She has not my suspicious, inquisitive eye, and would see it as the ivory tower, so to speak – and admirably plain – that housed a rare spirit. I'll grant it was unique; and Gilbert Osmond was unlike any man she had ever met.

They tempted her there, he and that Madame Merle – oh yes: quite deliberately, and in this his sister, Countess Gemini, agrees with me. By then Serena Merle knew about the legacy old Mr Touchett had left his niece. She'd liked Isabel well enough when she met her in England – who wouldn't? – and this sudden wealth made her (oh – dangerously!) the perfect creature to serve up to her precious Osmond.

But there I go, beginning in the middle: quite wrong for any narrative form – not that I'd dream of writing up such a story for the *Interviewer*, however much my readers back home would love it. Oh no: it was too near and too tragic – and who knows how it will end...

But how did it start? Madame Merle had certainly talked of him – and an excellent talker she was – when they met at Gardencourt during Mr Touchett's final illness. No doubt she had described this other-worldly, cultivated, sensitive widower and his little daughter just enough to intrigue an innocent heiress on her first trip to Europe. That may sound patronising, for Isabel is so very bright; and, granted, it was *my* first visit too – but, as a working girl and a hardened journalist, I knew so much more about the world. Be that as it may, Madame Merle must have sold the attractions of her rich novice to Osmond, for he roused himself from his exquisite isolation and travelled down to Florence to call on them at Mrs Touchett's palazzo when they they were both staying there during that first glorious May.

Preceding pages: *Gilbert Osmond's Florentine villa, a rather forbidding rectangle of weathered stone and stucco, flanked by cypresses.*

Opposite: *The elegant antechamber strikes one as strangely chill, despite the high arches and red-tiled floor.*

Isabel had seen little yet of the new continent, but even in Britain I noticed she was changing: she was losing her true-blue American values amid the insidious magic of the old world. Those decaying civilisations seemed to rub away some of that precious bloom and clear-sightedness that is so peculiarly transatlantic. Well, here in the capital of the depraved old Medicis – a climate capable of spawning such extremes as Fra Angelico and Machiavelli (as I said in my *Interviewer* piece) – she encountered the most exquisite taste and the most ingenious subtlety all combined in one man; and she was fascinated. Naturally Osmond invited her back to see his "humble abode"; and eagerly – and far too trustingly, for all her wit – she went. If only I had been there then: I would have warned her.

Gilbert Osmond's villa lies to the north of Florence. You drive out through the *Porta Romana* (Roman Gate) and uphill along winding lanes between high walls. I went later, with the Countess Gemini: she said his collection was "too amazing" and I should get an article out of it – but really, of course, I wanted to visit the scene of the crime, so to speak; to try and see for myself what other elements could have so fatally beguiled my dear friend in a man whom I could never begin to like. Well, as I have implied, the place has indeed a certain magic, even to me with my cold reviewer's eye. (When I reported on this to Mr Bantling, he quipped, "So she worshipped the ground he trod on!" But that's his brand of British fun.)

Anyway: near the crest you come out into a little irregular piazza, along one side of which lies the villa: a rather forbidding rectangle of weathered stone and stucco, flanked by cypresses. To be fair, it does not present its most appealing aspect to first view, being so very plain, private and fortress-like; but once inside the great *portone* one must concede the charm of the high, light court, with its arches and bright flowers. The building is clearly very old, and not truly modernised by American standards, but still a fine workable place, and clearly – one might say ostentatiously – the home of a collector. Alas: now my dear Isabel too is just another of his fine pieces...

It may have been a purely emotional reaction, but the antechamber struck me as chill, despite the note of colour in its red-tiled floor. There was something so

Opposite: *Like some private museum the villa is positively stuffed with* objets d'art, *all of which, as Osmond's sister pointed out, he had cleverly collected over the years.*

Left: *How different the restrained taste of the collector to the lobby of our hotel in Rome!*

Left: *Florence's* Porta Romana – *Roman Gate – through which you drive out of the city and along winding uphill lanes to reach the secluded villa.*

consciously well-arranged about it – but I must remind myself I had already met and taken against Osmond. On a more practical note, moreover, I was coming into shade out of hot sun. The drawing room was more *simpatico*: a fine, large apartment lit by three of the great architectural windows that face onto the piazza, and very comfortable, even luxurious, with easy chairs and a handsome modern desk. Otherwise it was like some private museum, positively stuffed with *objets d'arts* which, as I understood from his sister, he had collected very cleverly over the years. "He has had little money, but always a good eye," she said: "he delights in spotting and picking up the lesser works of the greater masters – and he finds them in the most unpromising places, Miss Stackpole!" And she led me to a darling little sketch by Correggio – no less! – that he had discovered beneath some crude daub by a later hand. Well, I'm wild for Correggio, of course: my very favourite artwork in the *world* is that adorable Madonna and Child of his in the Uffizi – I never miss a visit to it if I'm in Florence. Imagine having a Correggio of one's own!

But there was art everywhere: faded wall-hangings of damask and tapestry, statues, figurines, busts and endless pictures. Many of the latter I found somewhat flat and angular: rather too primitive perhaps for my

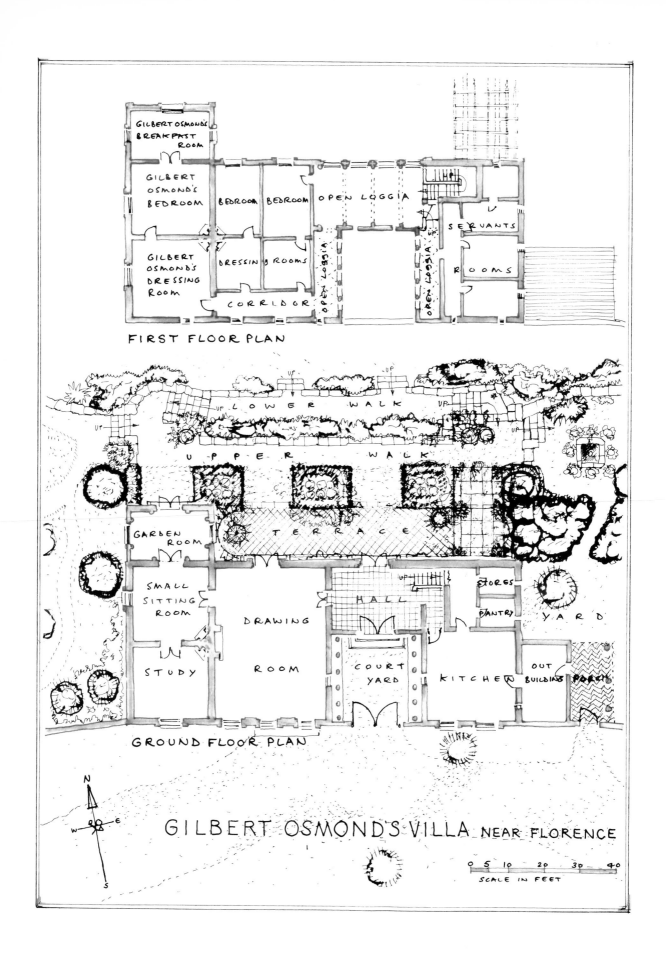

FIRST FLOOR PLAN

GILBERT OSMOND'S
BREAKFAST
ROOM

GILBERT
OSMOND'S
BEDROOM

BEDROOM

BEDROOM

OPEN LOGGIA

SERVANTS

GILBERT
OSMOND'S
DRESSING
ROOM

DRESSING ROOMS

OPEN LOGGIA

OPEN LOGGIA

ROOMS

CORRIDOR

LOWER WALK

UPPER WALK

GARDEN
ROOM

TERRACE

SMALL
SITTING
ROOM

DRAWING

HALL

STORES

PANTRY

YARD

STUDY

ROOM

COURT
YARD

KITCHEN

OUT
BUILDING

PORCH

GROUND FLOOR PLAN

GILBERT OSMOND'S VILLA NEAR FLORENCE

N

W   E

S

0 5 10   20   30   40
SCALE IN FEET

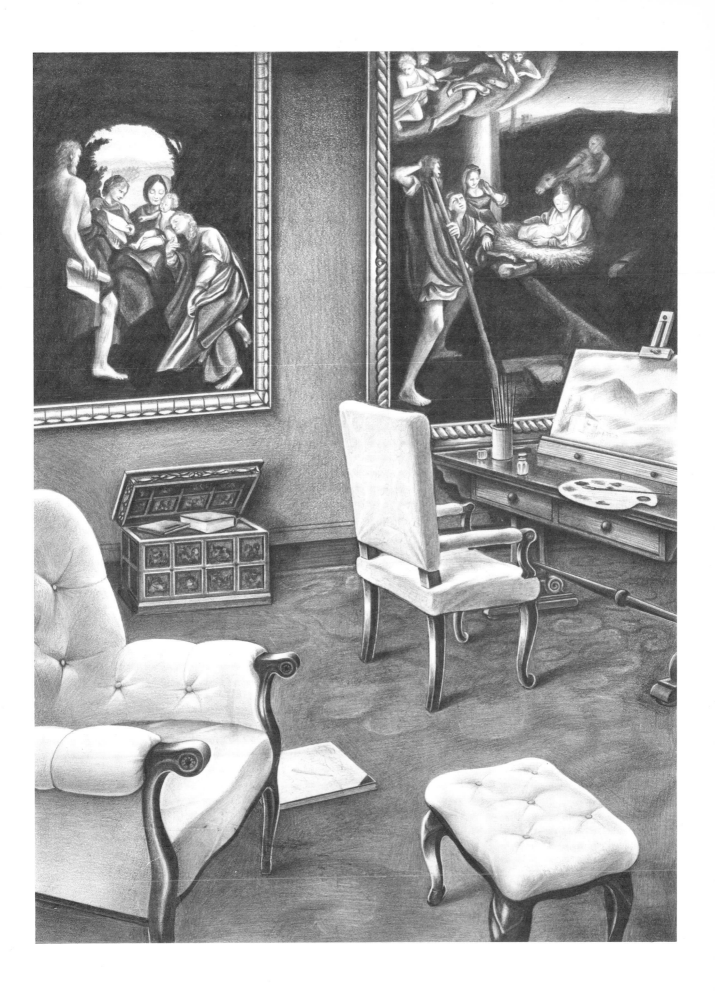

taste, and displayed very pedantically in crude, over-heavy frames – at least he might have touched up that worn gilt! For he could paint too: it was one of his accomplishments, and he even set out his own water-colour sketches on an easel there for general admiration. You see, he had no *real* occupation, but seemed to think a "talent for living" was sufficient.

There were more odd knicknacks, books and magazines than necessary, covering shelves and tables and even the velvet cushions that topped the great *cassones* (carved Italian chest or cabinets, originally wedding chests) that stood beneath the windows. There were numberless relics of brass and pottery with no real charm except I suppose to the antiquarian eye, being mere fragments of lost ornament, shards that defy dusting.

But apart from this obscure clutter, it was an impressive, even beautiful, room; two more were beyond, one with a piano, and both full of hangings and busts and pictures and rugs. I wondered what it must have been like for his little motherless daughter coming home from the convent to this one-man museum: it can't have been much fun for a child – and when I think of the amenities and pleasures for young folk back home, I don't wonder that she was rather an odd, formal little personage, somewhat lacking in spirit; over-eager to please – and quite disconcertingly observant. Totally devoted to Osmond, of course: his decorative little slave, as graceful – and almost as quiet – as any of his tasteful bronzes.

The chief virtue of the villa was the view over the Arno valley; and doors led from the drawing room onto a terrace pleasantly shady, though somewhat overgrown with tangled roses and vines that made me itch for the pruning shears. The ancient stone balustrade was a convenient height to lean on to admire the view; from one corner, if you craned out, you could just see the *Duomo* (cathedral) itself: not so fine a dome as that of our own Capitol in Washington, but excellently lit in the afternoon sunlight. Below us the ground fell away in hillsides of neat vines and olive

Opposite: The villa has a wonderful view over the valley of the Arno and, from one corner, of Florence itself. The terrace is pleasantly shady, though somewhat overgrown.

groves: little waste of space, agriculturally speaking; small holdings dotted around, with those pretty red-tiled roofs that are so very Mediterranean.

Upstairs, the Countess told me, were bedrooms and dressing rooms connected to the servants' wing by a loggia or covered way – those pleasant arches again. The villa was somewhat gentler in aspect from this side, and I can see why darling Isabel was charmed and intrigued. Yet I could not throw off my initial impression of calculated taste: I caught the odour of what I most detest: a "pose", that of the highminded expatriate recluse rejecting not just his own fine country, America, but the world itself, as too rough and ordinary for so delicate a spirit. Here in his eyrie, looking down on that world, he could make his life a work of art, with nothing so vulgar as a profession or an involvement with ordinary mortals to disturb him: concerned only with form. Form was his obsession.

But he was not such a recluse that he did not require admiration for his exclusivity; the grand gesture of self-denial is sweeter with witnesses – even if the world is brutishly unaware it has been rejected.

The irony is that Osmonds's much-vaunted gift for rare acquisitions ran riot, grew coarse, once he had Isabel's riches to play with: their Palazzo Roccanegra in Rome was very over-done by him: all florid and French Empire. She gave him a free hand; she took no part in it – and one could see that: it was so consciously grand; it quite lacked her naturalness and warmth. As Pansy said, rather touchingly I thought: "It's father's taste: he has so much of it."

Another irony – my last, I promise – is that they never returned to live in the villa where Isabel saw him, and fell in love with the man whose confined circumstances had produced such a cultured pearl of a dwelling. Not fancy enough for him, I guess.

GEORGE ELIOT

(1819 – 1880)

Born Mary Ann Evans in Warwickshire on November 22 1819, George Eliot spent her childhood in the country, the daughter of a land agent. A plain girl, she had exceptional intelligence and character, attributes which won the respect of many throughout her life.

Educated in Coventry, George Eliot developed an ardent interest in religion, joining, at different times, the evangelical and Unitarian churches. In 1836, her mother died and George Eliot looked after her father at home, occupying her time by learning Italian and German, reading and playing music. In 1841 she moved to Coventry and fell in with a circle of Unitarian friends. She worked for three years on a translation of Levi-Stauss' *Leben Jesu* which was published in 1846, and after her father's death she travelled to Europe, spending several months in Geneva.

On returning to London, she worked for a publishing house and edited articles for the *Westminster* magazine. It was in London that she met George Henry Lewes, a married man, linguist and literary critic and in 1854 she travelled abroad with him and became his constant companion. Discarded by several friends as a result of this arrangement, Eliot was encouraged by Lewes to write and in 1856 began *Scenes from a Clerical Life*. She gained critical acclaim and became much admired by literary circles and the common populace alike. Eliot continued to write and eventually moved with Lewes to Witley in Surrey. In 1871 she wrote *Middlemarch*, followed by *Daniel Deronda* in 1874. Lewes died four years later and after some time, Eliot married John Walter Cross, a friend for several years. She died in December 1880.

Chapter 3
MIDDLEMARCH

"It had a small park, with a fine old oak here and there, and an avenue of limes towards the south west front, with a sunk fence between park and pleasure ground, so that from the drawing-room windows the glance swept uninterruptedly along a slope of greensward till the limes ended in a level of corn and pastures, which often seemed to melt into a lake under the setting sun. This was the happy side of the house, for the south and east looked rather melancholy even under the brightest morning."

Joshua Smith has been clock-winder to the gentry in the flourishing Midlands town of Middlemarch for exactly fifty years, inheriting the position from his father, whom he would accompany on his rounds from the age of thirteen. (As regular readers of this column will know, any names – and only the names – are fictional, including those of his employers and their respective mansions: aspiring intruders and sight-seers please take note!) I have chosen to make him the subject of this week's *Short & Simple Annals* as I am persuaded, not only that he is a great "character", but that his access as a trusted, skilled and indeed familiar employee in the finer houses of the district will appeal to our feminine readers as well.

Joshua Smith – Maestro Smith, one might say, as this master-horologist and homespun philosopher also plays the violin – lives in a small neat dwelling near the old centre of Middlemarch from which he travels, by horseback in summer and a small trap in winter, to outlying villages and estates to service the time-pieces of such great houses as Stone Court, Tipton Grange, Freshitt Hall and Lowick Manor. He rises betimes to work on the watches and small clocks he brings home with him – though he tells me that now his eyes are growing weaker and tend to water in the mornings, he is beginning to spend the early hours tending to his garden in spring, summer and autumn, using the equivalent time in the winter months making and mending; his good wife's cooking pots, new canes for his fine old rocking-chair, even steaming ply-wood for a home-made violin. A man of parts: a man for all seasons.

But he insists I tell of the household he travels to: "they are far more worthy of your readers' attention," he says. "The Grange at Tipton, now: Mr Brookes' residence, and his two young nieces, Miss Dorothea and Miss Celia with him… Ah, but they both were wed within the last two years. Miss Celia, the younger – an easy, pleasant little lady, if I may be so bold – made a good marriage to Sir James Chettam of Freshitt Hall nearby, though rumour had it he courted the elder Miss Brookes first. But she, a handsome, high-minded young lady – not the sort that bothers about mere appearances and trinkets, if

Preceding pages: *Lowick Manor, home of the Reverend Edward Casaubon and his young bride. A great old house, its most outstanding feature is the avenue of limes stretching from the south-west front.*

you know what I mean – was determined to marry that dry old bachelor, the Reverend Edward Casaubon—" (He apologised at this juncture for such severity about his betters; who was he to judge? etc – but I assured him I was changing all the names, and it was not "gossip" but "human interest", after all.)

"It wasn't his money she was after, either, nor that great grey house, Lowick Manor, where he had lived with his mother and, since her death, lived on alone. No, I do believe the young lady admired his mind, sir, and wanted to espouse and assist in his Great Work of Scholarship, the Key to All the Mythologies; in a word, to Do Good – rather than 'do well'.

"It seemed an odd match, and not just to your humble servant, but to many more knowledgable folk – especially considering that a young lord was wooing her at the same time, with Freshitt and all its pleasant acres to lay at her feet. For Freshitt Hall is a fine and delightful country house, as different as could be from Lowick: newer and elegant classical, with its white columns and broad flagged pavement and sloping terraces full of roses. Well, Miss Celia – Lady Chettam, I should say – was very happy to pick up what her sister rejected, and now has a fine little boy, I hear. Mrs Casaubon is a model wife to a –" (he sought for the careful word, this time) – "a *difficult* husband, as I think I may fairly call him; working with him in that dark old library early and late. You know, I do not believe that dear young lady knows the meaning of the term 'self-interest'. And I must admit it is the remarkable sweetness, and true charity, of the Mistress of Lowick that makes her so well loved throughout the district, and my humble visits there notable occasions for me – rather than the quality and interest of the time-pieces or the grandeur of the Manor itself.

"It is not a beautiful place – though, filled with children and flowers and music and merry-making, it could be. For it is a great old house, austerely built in grey stone some two hundred years ago; and I can vouch it has not been altered, improved or refurbished in *my* lifetime. My father used to say that when old Mrs Casaubon, the Reverend's late mother, first came there as a bride, she had all the rooms new decorated; she brought a deal of that pretty tip-toe frenchie furniture with her – you know, sir, all gilt and brocade: made him feel a careless touch would send it toppling, he said. That was mostly in the great drawing room and the old lady's boudoir above it; and silk on the walls, you know, and the chinese vases and

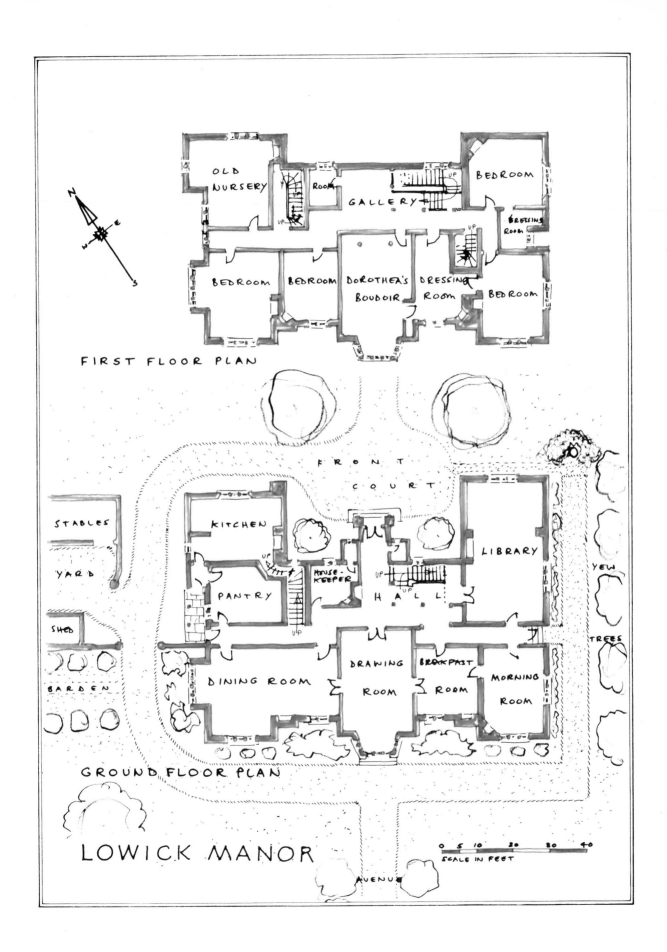

FIRST FLOOR PLAN

OLD NURSERY
ROOM
GALLERY
BEDROOM
DRESSING ROOM
BEDROOM
BEDROOM
DOROTHEA'S BOUDOIR
DRESSING ROOM
BEDROOM

FRONT COURT

STABLES
YARD
KITCHEN
LIBRARY
YEW
SHED
PANTRY
HOUSE-KEEPER
HALL
TREES
GARDEN
DINING ROOM
DRAWING ROOM
BREAKFAST ROOM
MORNING ROOM

GROUND FLOOR PLAN

LOWICK MANOR

0 5 10 20 30 40
SCALE IN FEET

AVENUE

41

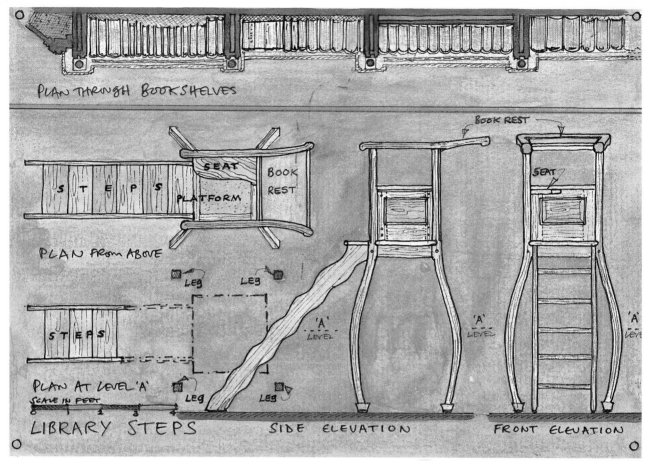

PLAN THROUGH BOOKSHELVES

S T E P S

PLATFORM

SEAT

BOOK REST

PLAN FROM ABOVE

LEG   LEG

S T E P S

PLAN AT LEVEL 'A'

SCALE IN FEET

LEG   LEG

LIBRARY STEPS

BOOK REST

SEAT

'A' LEVEL

SIDE ELEVATION

'A' LEVEL

'A' LEVEL

FRONT ELEVATION

ornaments, all very fine: the best, and all antiques. But queerly lifeless, if you catch my meaning: frozen – like in their same positions over the years; dusted and put back just so.

"And young Mrs Casaubon has not changed a single item, it seems; as if to say: I am happy with your mother's arrangements and shall alter nothing. As I remarked earlier, she was not concerned with possessions – only with actions: to achieve some good in her life. Even in our brief, and very cordial, conversations, I receive this impression of a power to do great things; yet sadly unemployed, like a perfectly designed watch, clean and oiled and wound – then left lying in the dark drawer of some heavy old cabinet, just waiting to be used, to work, to be relied upon. . .

"But I am being fanciful now: the indulgence of an old man. As I say, I always enjoy my visits there. In the old days I used to go over and wind the clocks once a week: the long-case in the entrance hall, the Boulle in the library, the fancy French piece – most tuneful – in the drawing room, the marble clock in the blue boudoir, and so on. Recently Mrs Casaubon has taken it upon herself to do the weekly winding: 'It is a long way for you to come in all weathers, Mr. Smith, for a half-hour's service,' she said, 'if, under your thorough

Above: A huge brown room lined with musty books, the library is where the Casaubons work at opposite desks.

Opposite: The boudoir overlooking the avenue had belonged to Reverend Casaubon's late mother. Dorothea had not changed a single thing, being unconcerned with possessions, and far more absorbed in plans for the new hospital.

instruction, it is one I could perform; and if you will continue to visit monthly and keep an eye on them. I must add there is no question of your losing financially by such an arrangement: it is simply a way of putting both your time and mine to better use – and Time is your business after all, is it not?' And she laughed as she rarely does, and put her arm through mine. 'This week I want you to advise me about the wall clock in the housekeeper's parlour: a Benson of London, I believe. Tantripp my maid says its tick sounds oddly muffled – "woolly" was the word she used – and that the housekeeper harbours dark suspicions of a nesting mouse! And fears to sit in the room till you have investigated.'

"We were, I recall, passing along the broad, dark-panelled corridor that leads past the library to the

great entrance hall. A door opened and the Reverend Mr Casaubon stood there, gaunt and forbidding like some old deaths-head in the gloom. He must have been disturbed by the sound of her laughter; and now he summoned his wife peremptorily into the library. I heard him remark – and no doubt was intended to hear – 'Dorothea, you will please me not to be so easy with the tradesmen.'

"That library is a sad place: a huge brown room lined with musty books. They work at two desks facing each other, and there is also a great table laid out with notebooks on the Great Work – rows of them, like so many tombstones. The drawing room, with its bow window that opens out onto a terrace, is pleasant but it is seldom used, and looks so: very formal, in red and white and gold. It is the boudoir above it, also with a bow window looking down along the lime tree walk, that Mrs Casaubon seems to like the best, and sits there when not working in the library. It is a spacious room, and brighter, being on the first floor;

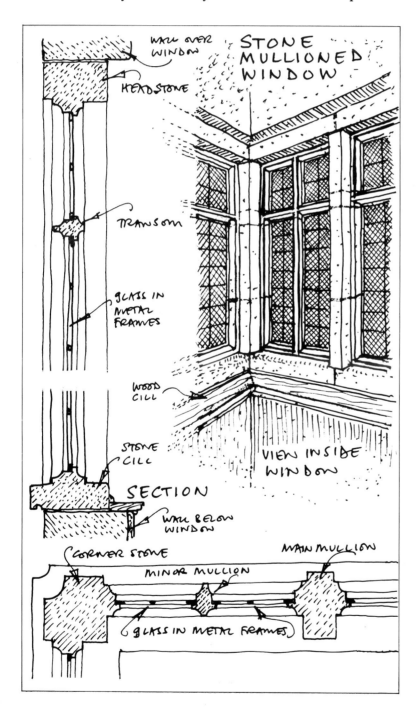

indeed the sun comes in on this side, away from all those funereal yews and box hedges that surround so much of the Manor – and the faded blue furnishings are both elegant and restful.

"There is a charming old tapestry over the door, and a group of miniatures I always pause to study when I visit the apartment to attend to the clocks, (a small carriage and the plain marble). One portrait in particular holds my eye, of a lady with powdered hair, and a pretty but irregular and most interesting face. Tantripp informed me it was a likeness of the Reverend's great aunt: 'the black sheep of the family', says she – I am certain she overdoes the story! – who made an unsuitable marriage and was rejected by her relatives; and more, about her daughter, I think, and a penniless Polish artist. 'But there is a striking family resemblance, is there not?' I ventured, 'with that young cousin, the artistic youth whom Mr Casaubon treats so generously—' 'Generously? Pshaw!' says she: 'young Ladislaw gets only his due rights, people say; and Mr Casaubon has no liking for him. I'd go so far as to say he is something more than jealous of his young cousin.' Well, I do not know about such things, of course: I see the lady of the house, and enter her boudoir to attend to her clocks, not to speculate on her family connections. . .

"As I was saying, she has not altered the room: it as her late mother-in-law left it – except that now it is a 'working-room'. Her table is spread with plans for the new hospital, and her own sketches for improved workmen's cottages; there are German and Latin grammars, too, to help her with her husband's scholarly studies – no feminine frippery in sight, no embroidery or novelettes or sheets of music; indeed there is only one harpsichord in the whole of that great manor, and it is covered up with books. . .

"But 'female frippery' puts me in mind of another house – even more different from Lowick than the Chettam place, to my way of seeing. This is a house in Lowick Gate, on the edge of Middlemarch, that is, leading towards the Manor and church. It is quite lately that I have started visiting Doctor Lydgate's, and, while again the residence of a newly-wed couple, it is the diametrical opposite in almost every way. It is such variety that has always been the very spice of my odd calling.

"Here, now, we have as handsome a young couple as you could wish: Doctor Tertius Lydgate is from a fine old family – though not as wealthy, I understand, as in the past (without any intimation, believe me, of having fallen on hard times.) Oh no: on the contrary, everything Doctor Lydgate chooses or, indeed, has inherited, is of the best; and he clearly likes it that way – so far as he concerns himself with such matters. For he is high-minded – not unlike Mrs Casaubon in his mission to improve the world through study and service. He has the advantage of a highly-trained practical intelligence, an energetic sense of purpose and a masculine determination that may achieve great things, may take him far – if the alarming novelty and uncompromising idealism of his plans do not antagonise the Old School: the so-called Establishment I mean, sir. He has taken as a wife the very prettiest, most accomplished young lady in the town – and I say 'the town' advisedly: her father is in trade, her fond family very comfortably off; but not what one might call Top Drawer, d'you see?

"Their house, now. Well, it is not their own, but rented; fine and quite large, and set in a very respected part of Middlemarch. After all, an aspiring physician could not be expected, without a considerable private income, to consider purchasing such a place; and if he'd been a son of mine I'd have said, Start Smaller, lad, and save towards your own dwelling, however humble. But you can understand how he wanted to please – and to show off to best advantage – his lovely bride; and (though for himself he might not care, being accustomed to Family Seats) to give her a fine place to play with, so to speak, and occupy her time.

"So he has his profession whilst she has her dollshouse – and how prettily and elaborately she has furnished it! No cheese-paring, no nip-and-tuck there – oh no! She has the pianoforte and the buttoned sofas and the pleated silk worktables and the elegant gilt looking-glasses, the flounced drapes and the shawls, nets and laces – all spanking new, it seems, and in the very latest of fashions. You cannot but admire all the new plate and sets of glasses on display. Only the clock in the servants' hall is old; but those in the drawing room and dining room, and the handsome inlaid long-case in the hall, really do not need my services; and I cannot but feel it is more of a formality, visiting the Lydgate household to wind their time-pieces: as though little Mistress Rosamund (whom I have known from a babe in arms) considers it 'proper' that I should call there regularly as I do at Freshitt and Tipton Grange.

"But why should *I* complain? Little Miss Rosie Vincey has become a grand young lady now – with aristocratic connections, as she seldom lets one forget

– and she must have her way. She certainly wears the most elegant dresses and the most artfully-coiffed hair in Middlemarch, and entertains company, and keeps a generous number of servants. Doctor Lydgate is perfectly delighted with her, I am sure; and, working so hard and such long hours on many unremunerative projects like the new hospital and all his scientific studies meanwhile, he leaves the decisions and arrangements to his wife. (His bill for my services is outstanding; I am sure that does not signify – but I do find it uncomfortable to speak of financial matters to Mrs Lydgate, you see: she is usually entertaining her lady-friends or busy singing duets with some elegant young sprig when I call, and sends the maid to deal with me).

"Oh yes indeed: a simple clock-winder like myself sees a lot on his weekly rounds, and may be forgiven

Above: *Very much the residence of a newly-married couple, this comfortable town house in Lowick Gate, on the edge of Middlemarch, is rented by aspiring physician Doctor Tertius Lydgate and his wife.*

Opposite: *The drawing room. Here Mistress Rosamund, encouraged by her doting husband, has indulged her passion for elaborate furnishings, everything spanking new and in the very latest fashion.*

for falling into philosophising at times about his employers... You know, sir, I find that, for all her finery and curlicues and spanking new case, the Doctor's lady-wife emits a curiously tinny note; while the plainer and somewhat sombre marble of Mrs Casaubon strikes a deep, true, bell-like tone, that touches my fond old heart."

COUNT LEO TOLSTOY

(1828 – 1910)

Leo Tolstoy was the fourth son of Count and Countess Tolstoy of Yasnaya Polyana. He spent his early childhood on the family estate and at the age of nine moved to Moscow. After his father and grandmother died, Tostoy enrolled at Kazan University where he began reading Diplomacy and subsequently changed to Law, but neither subject satisfied him and in 1847 he left the university before completing his course.

In 1851 Tolstoy inherited the estate of Yasnaya Polyana and four years later joined the Imperial Army in the Caucasus and the Crimea. He travelled to Paris and Switzerland and by 1860 was teaching peasants on his family estate to read and write while both writing and acting as estate administrator. He wrote an educational review, and in 1862 married Sophie Andreyeva Behrs, a girl very much his junior. Spurred on by the birth of a son, Tolstoy wrote *War and Peace* and *Anna Karenin*. Though he loved his wife, Tolstoy was a difficult and temperamental man. His idealism gained him both admirers and critics, and led to his excommunication by the Russian Holy Synod in 1901.

He died in 1910 at Astapovo.

Chapter 4

WAR AND PEACE

"He got up and went to the window to open it. As soon as he drew the shutters the moonlight flooded the room as though it had long been waiting at the window. He unfastened the casement. The still night was cool and beautiful. Just outside the window was a row of pollard-trees, looking black on one side and silvery bright on the other. Under the trees grew some sort of lush, wet, bushy vegetation with leaves and stems touched here and there with silver. Farther away, beyond the dark trees, a roof glittered with dew; to the right was a great, leafy tree with satiny white trunk and branches, and above it shone the moon, almost full, in a pale, practically starless, spring sky. Prince Andrei leaned his elbows on the window ledge, and his eyes gazed at the heavens."

Sitting here by the study fire at Bald Hills, in that same great room where the old Prince Bolkonsky used to keep all his worktables and lathes, his half-written memoirs and mathematical tomes – all shoved away in the attics now, I shouldn't wonder – it is odd to look back over the past fifteen years or so and see by what tortuous routes we have all arrived here, and now live at peace. Nikolai, Princess Maria, Pierre, Natasha – yes, and Cousin Sonya too; there is a place for her, as there has always been: a good girl, an excellent woman. And finally, of course, myself, Vasili Denisov.

"Darling Denisov!" How clearly I can still hear that welcoming cry. It was the first time Nikolai Rostov came home on leave, and I accompanied him. Natasha's voice was always, it seemed, on the edge of laughter in those days; she darted across the great ballroom of the Moscow house and threw her dear skinny arms round my neck and kissed me: my introduction to the Rostov household! I confess that, although she can't have been more than thirteen or fourteen then, I was not a little in love with her. She was dark-haired and black-eyed; very slight and boyish of figure, like a young charioteer. (Maria Dmitrevna, *le terrible dragon* of the old school – imperial blood, no less, in her veins, and a terror to all – had a remarkably soft spot for little Natasha: "Well – and how's my Cossack?" she would boom. She liked the spirit of the girl: the way she stood up to the *grand dame's* bullying banter, where strong men would quail and take refuge in the card-room.)

And the morning after our arrival when we slept so late, Nikolai and I. His rooms were down on the ground floor; and I was only half awake when the servants brought in washbasins and hot water – already they must have polished our boots and brushed up our clothes from the adjoining room: a veritable chaos of sabres and bags, open portmanteaus, sabretaches and discarded uniforms – when we became aware of rustling and laughter and clanking, and then faces at the door as Petya and Natasha burst in to wake up their lazy brother and his comrade-at-arms. He chased them off, and we hurriedly put on dressing gowns – and there in the anteroom was little Petya wielding a sabre, and Natasha with one great spurred boot on and pulling up the other; and Sonya, the pretty cousin, pirouetting to make her skirt puff out like a balloon – what a scene! What chattering and questioning, and never giving us time to answer as they swept us

Opposite: *The great house on Povarsky Street, considered one of the finest in Moscow society, home of the Rostovs. Here the Count and his family lived comfortably and entertained on a lavish scale, regardless of cost.*

through to the sitting room for coffee – It may seem silly enough now, but, you know, I had not felt such a sunshine of well-being and affection since I joined the army some eighteen months before. I can remember how I found I simply couldn't stop smiling foolishly, and felt my very soul expanding in that warm glow... Well, that gives you some impression of the household, the family, I discovered then, in the winter of 1806, and since that time have never lost sight of them: always been close, I believe, like an honorary elder cousin.

A comfortable and extravagant social life they led; carefree and prodigally generous. Count Rostov, and his "little countess", as he always called her, were inordinately fond of their four children (did I mention Vera, the eldest? A rather smug, disapproving young lady, I thought: made a boring marriage). They could refuse them nothing; and were fond and indulgent with their house-serfs, who worshipped them. The mansion in Povarsky Street – though not to be compared with the Bezuhov palace – was considered one of the finest in Moscow society, with its great staircase leading up to the main rooms: the drawing rooms, the ballroom and conservatory, the music room, the Count's study, the card room, the icon room, and so on.

The Count, a charming, portly little man – a great dancer – loved nothing more than good company, and entertained lavishly, organising and overseeing all the elaborate arrangements himself. But even in those days, as Nikolai discovered later and confided to me, his father was having money troubles, and remortgaging his estates to provide for his family and way of life; not just one household and army of dependants: there was the apartment in Petersburg, of course, and the great country house and estates of Otradnoe – his other love. And he would gather up his family and paraphenalia and sweep them off to this huge dacha – a country palace in itself – where they would all hunt and entertain and play music and go visiting; and he, rather ineffectually but very enthusiastically, would "see to" the management of his broad acres.

I always found him the best of companions. I think

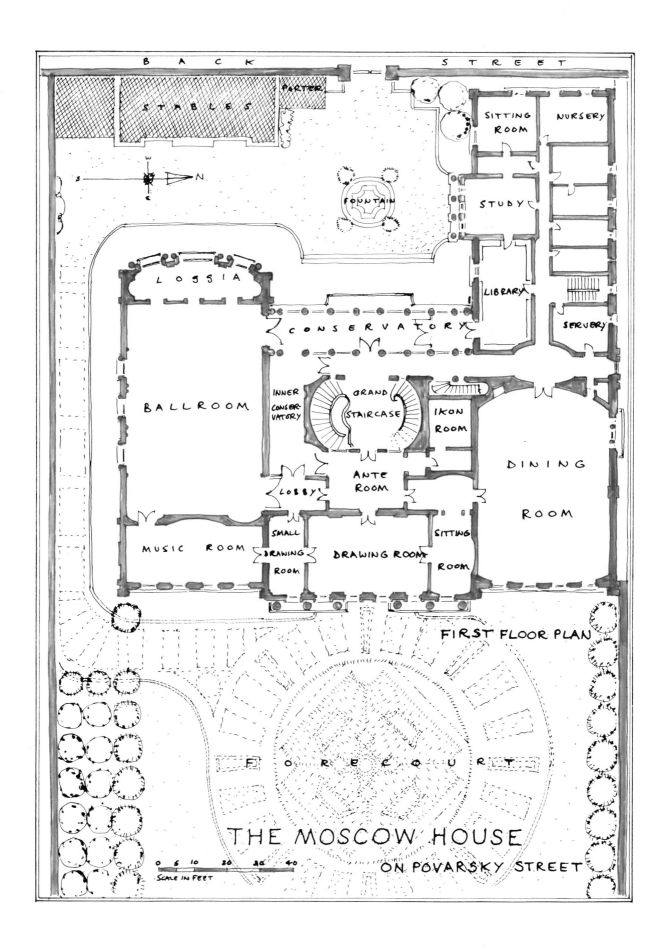

BACK STREET

STABLES

PORTER

SITTING ROOM

NURSERY

FOUNTAIN

STUDY

LIBRARY

SERVERY

LOGGIA

CONSERVATORY

INNER CONSERVATORY

GRAND STAIRCASE

IKON ROOM

BALLROOM

DINING ROOM

ANTE ROOM

LOBBY

MUSIC ROOM

SMALL DRAWING ROOM

DRAWING ROOM

SITTING ROOM

FIRST FLOOR PLAN

FORECOURT

THE MOSCOW HOUSE

ON POVARSKY STREET

0 5 10   20   30   40
SCALE IN FEET

52

I may say we got on well together, not only because I was Nikolai's friend, but perhaps because, deep down, we had much in common. For I myself – a retired general now, it is true – have never been an ambitious man: good company is enough for me. I know the younger folk regard me as a bit of a "bumbler", a bit of a comedy-figure, even: well-meaning, easy-going, wouldn't you say? But to be fair on myself, now, a perfectly adequate soldier – which has been my only career, and, thanks to the Emperor Napoleon, a busy one, not without its dangers and its tragedies – but the cameraderie made it all worthwhile...

What was I saying? Oh yes: Count Rostov, even before the war with the French, was – well, in hard economic terms, was running his very comfortable household at a loss. He and the Countess were too generous: greathearted but totally unaware of the value of money, I think; and when he did face the problem, he tried to protect her from such matters. Long afterwards – it must have been about 1813 – when the Count died, and the full extent of his muddles and debts were revealed to my dear Nikolai, he took over the burden and struggled on, attempting to pay those debts. He could have rejected the inheritance – but he would not dishonour his father's name. He could have stayed in the army, and so exempted by law – but he knew his mother needed him; and even *then* he protected the old Countess from the truth, from hardship and loss of face. So she continued as generous and extravagant, living in the happy past, while Niki, with Cousin Sonya's unquestioning assistance as a sort of companion-housekeeper, kept things running somehow. That was, so to speak, the Fall of the House of Rostov – a year after the fall of Moscow; and all the teeming, happy, turbulent life of the great mansion of Povarsky Street became just a memory.

Yet Moscow survived; and in the same way, that old life has been reborn, albeit in a changed, more purposeful form, here at Bald Hills. While I have been staying here with Nikolai and his Princess Maria (the saving of him: love *and* money!), with Natasha and her Pierre, and their respective children, it is only natural for me, a retired bachelor, to treasure those old memories; to take them out and turn them over, and see them glint in the light of past summers and chandeliers long broken or looted from vanished ballrooms. I salute the present, but I really have only the past – committed to no wife, no child, no stake in the future. And I say this without bitterness; though Cousin Sonya, whom I remember from the first visit as a lovely kitten of sixteen, shyer than little Natasha but rosy and laughing and playful – and, alas, terribly in love with Nikolai – I think that *she* may feel bitter, and that life has passed her by. I had the army, after all; but she has always been the poor relation, however pretty: the one that people turned to with their confidances, or some little job to be done; the one they relied on as a pillar of strength when times grew hard and servants few. And while I get great pleasure now from my proxy families and their good fortune, riding round with Nikolai to admire the crops or the new church he has built, or having young Andrusha climb on my knee and pull at my moustaches ("Darling Denisov!"), Cousin Sonya in the background, now a fading spinster, must feel that all these things could have been *hers*.

For she never wavered in her devotion to Nikolai. Fifteen years ago, when Natasha was busy falling in love with everybody – with Boris, with me (a little), with Prince Andrei – Sonya waited only for Nikolai. I know she turned down a proposal from the dashing Dolohov – yes, that was just before Iogel's ball, and it made her brighter and more confident as she stepped out onto the floor. That was an evening! Not the greatest, but always the most enjoyable of Moscow balls, for Iogel it was who had taught dancing to all that generation; and on this occasion had taken a ballroom in Bezuhov's house.

It was Natasha's very first ball – her first long dress: white with pink ribbons; I remember, and I was desperately in love with her then. Though I don't normally dance, I could not refuse her request to partner her in the Mazurka. Nikolai put her up to it, as I realised: he knew it was my one dance; and so I took the floor with her and – well, mine is the Polish, the *real* Mazurka, you see: not the dancing-master's version at all – and I believe I excelled myself. Really – not just an old duffer's tall story! But what a partner I had! – instinctively following and playing up to my cavortings.

And two days after that I proposed to her – proposals seemed to be in the air. I know I should have approached her parents first, but all at once I was quite carried away – this time by her singing: for Natasha had a lovely voice. I urged her to take it more seriously, to train and practise; and I would sit and listen to her by the hour... It was quite late, after the theatre and supper. We were in the music room, next door to the great drawing room where the Countess and some old friend were playing cards; Vera too, at the chessboard with Shinshin, I think; and Nikolai came in to listen. Sonya played the clavichord while Natasha sang my favourite barcarolle – And I was so overcome I offered her my heart and hand – and felt so ashamed of myself, such a fool, when Natasha returned with her mother and gracefully refused. She was far too young, as the Countess explained; and she was not really in love...

Such recollections are far clearer to me than those first years of the war. I think it must have been Schön Graben that was the first real battle young Nikolai was involved in – and wounded too. The French had crossed the bridge at Vienna, and General Kutuzov learnt through spies and outriders that the enemy was advancing in strength to cut off our lines of communication. We had to move fast, and engaged in battle while our troops were still weary.

But if young Rostov thought that was the war, he – and we all – had no notion of what was to follow. Napoleon's Grand Army was (and as a professional soldier I appreciate this) a most marvellous machine. We may have been scornful of the Austrians at Ulm, surrounded and capitulating without a fight; and surprised at the routing of the brave Prussians and Napoleon's ruthless pursuit of them across northern Germany; but Schön Graben gave us a taste of it, and Austerlitz, Jena and the terrible winter campaign, where both sides lost so many, were still to come. It was only after Friedland that our beloved Tsar signed a treaty with Napoleon at Tilsit, and Russia was finally at peace.

"Finally"! The worst was still hidden in the future: the little Emperor had not finished yet. Diverted by campaigns in Spain, where our erstwhile allies the English were fighting him, he turned his attentions our way once more in the summer of 1812 when Tsar Alexander rejoined the Allies. Six hundred thousand men – think of it: the greatest army in history! –

Opposite: *The ballroom, its chandelier muffled, card tables pushed back against the walls, awaits the French invasion.*

Below: *The icon room. Few remain, as the best pieces were packed when the family left the city before the advancing French.*

Above: *Uncle's hunting lodge, on the Otradnoe estate –*
and marvellous evenings they had there after a day's
hunting, dancing to balalaika and guitar!

Napoleon led into our land. And the speed at which
that army could march! The fall of Smolensk, the loss
of the Shevardino redoubt – all happened so quickly!
Then two days later, the battle of Borodino: our
very last line of defence between Moscow and the
Grand Army.

No: I'm not going start on Borodino again, though,
as you know – or perhaps I didn't tell you? – I, Vasili
Dmitrich Denisov, actually went to General Kutuzov
with my Master Plan. Yes: and guerilla warfare was
the key. "Give me five hundred men," I told him,
"and I'll surprise them and cut their line of supply."
But though the great man listened, and looked at my
diagrams and maps, he really took no notice... I *know*
it was a good plan; and Prince Andrei Bolkonsky was
impressed by it, I think. That was the first time I'd
actually met him, you know, though we'd both heard
about each other from the Rostovs. Funny to think
we'd both been in love with Natasha; though I
suppose I can't really compare my absurd declaration
– and a devotion, mark you, that has never ceased –
with that great romantic encounter, dancing at the
Emperor's ball in St Petersburg.

She was sixteen or seventeen by then; the Prince
already widowed, a coming man in diplomatic and
army circles. The Rostovs were delighted and
honoured to give his proposal their blessing; and
Natasha accepted him. She was in awe of him, I think,
as well as in love: she simply couldn't believe at first a
man like that – so wise, so serious: whom even her
papa listened to – could be hers... But his father, the
old Prince – yes, the eccentric old bear who used to
rule this house with a rod of iron – he wasn't so
pleased; he said they must not marry for a year. Poor
little Natasha! To be given the world one moment,
and then have it taken away from her and put on a high
shelf, so to speak: to be told she must "wait for it", like
a good child.

So Prince Andrei went off, and – well, you know
what happened in that year of waiting. Or maybe you
don't: Pierre Bezuhov and the Rostovs between them
pretty well shut it up. But that scoundrel Anatole
Kuragin flirted outrageously with the girl and turned
her head so she thought she must be in love with *him*.

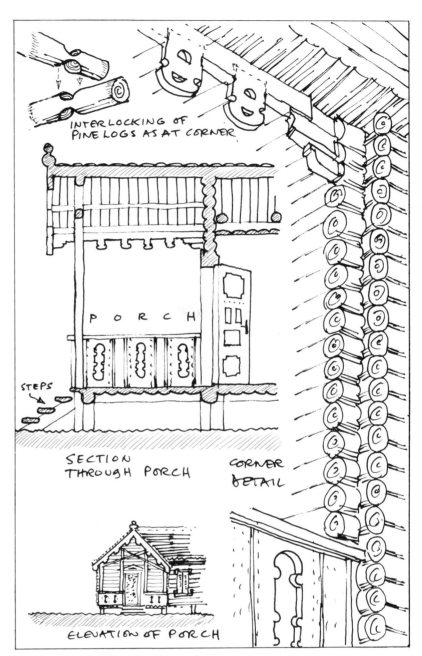

INTERLOCKING OF
PINE LOGS AS AT CORNER

P O R C H

STEPS

SECTION
THROUGH PORCH

CORNER
DETAIL

ELEVATION OF PORCH

Right: *The hunting lodge belonging to Mihail Nikanorovich, known to the young Rostovs as "Uncle", was the scene of much merriment.*

There was even talk of an attempted elopement – not that he intended to marry her – he had one wife already, did Anatole... Anyway, the engagement with the Prince was broken off. No wonder he was looking so sad when we talked of our "mutual friends" in Moscow and Petersburg. And a few days later it was, at Borodino, he was desperately wounded.

What a disaster that battle was: if we had engaged with the Russians sooner, on a better terrain— By the end of it, I believe, so many of our men had been slaughtered that the survivors were outnumbered two to one. Yet they say that it was never an outright victory for the French on account of the fact that

Napoleon's genius was fogged by a head-cold that day: the Russians could have been wiped out, and the world's history changed... As it was, the remains of our army retreated to Moscow and beyond. Most of the inhabitants had already fled; certainly our Tsar had left.

But history will show that though the French won the battle, we – one might say, Mother Russia – won the campaign. And though Kutozov was accused of abandoning Moscow without a battle, he knew that to engage against those odds would have lost both Moscow and the Russian army: he chose instead to save the army at least, and fight when the time was

ripe. His was a wily peasant cunning, allied with that dogged resistance and determination to survive, that is the character of our people.

Just imagine the moment when the Emperor Napoleon achieved his goal and reached out to grasp his glittering prize: all Moscow with its golden cupolas, its palaces, its thousand churches, its wealth, was his. But he was playing by the rules: strict protocol, as with Vienna; moreover he would be magnanimous and fair in victory; create a new and better order of society, a reformed code of law... He waited for the official delegation: for the keys of the city, the tray of bread and salt that symbolised surrender, welcome – and he waited in vain. No one remained in Moscow except the one-fiftieth, the dregs of society: no governor, official, nor local dignitary, but thieves, looters and rabble, prisoners let loose from the gaols, lunatics from the asylum, and those too poor or sick to move themselves.

So the French moved in; very orderly at first, no looting or burning – and pitched camp in the great squares. But what a cornucopia of supplies, what houses, what comfort, what abundance of wine, of fine carriages, of art treasures, of gold were there for the taking, in an abandoned capital! And gradually they fanned out, dug in, made themselves at home. They missed the evening roll-call... Over five weeks, discipline went to pieces: they enjoyed the rich billet, living well and carelessly, using up supplies that could have kept even the Grand Army through the winter. Then there were the fires: no, Moscow was not deliberately burned – neither by the retreating Russians nor the invading French. It was a wooden city, and fire, common at the best of times, now started carelessly through horseplay or drinking and were not put out: *they* were not concerned to save property; they simply moved on to the next street.

I have heard a great deal of this at first hand from Pierre Bezuhov, who stayed there, half out of sheer curiosity, I think – I've never really understood that man – and half for the sake of a hare-brained plan to shoot the Emperor. He was taken prisoner for suspected arson, however, and nearly executed. As for me, I was entirely taken up with the new guerilla warfare: skirmishes through the outlying woods to cut

Previous pages: *The drawing room at Otradnoe, the Rostovs' country estate. More palace than dacha, here the family would hunt and entertain and go visiting while the Count would "see to" his broad acres.*

Opposite: *The hall at Otradnoe. Sledging and skating – those were the best times, before the threat of war clouded the lives of the Rostovs and those they loved.*

off small bands of the French, or get fresh horses for our troops, or free Russian prisoners. Ironically, it was on one of the latter expeditions that little Petya Rostov – Petya who had joined the army at fifteen! – was killed: I still cannot bring myself to think of it. And we discovered Pierre himself among the men we freed.

Pierre is the most philosophical of our little company here at Bald Hills; and he believes that the French army created its own downfall. If they had pursued and fought us after Borodino, or marched on St Petersburg, or even wintered in Moscow, who knows if Russia would not now be part of the French Empire? But they did nothing for five weeks: seduced, if you like, by that rich abandoned city. Perhaps Napoleon's error lay in complacency: he even sent an envoy to our general's camp to propose peace terms. "No settlement of any sort," was Kutozov's reply: *"Such is the spirit of my nation."* He knew the French army was falling apart, and he restrained his cossacks from battle until the right moment – yes: the Grand Army was leaving Moscow! With their carriages and their loot and their prisoners, it was like a nation on the move. There was mild October weather, an indian summer, when they set out, but they had some seven hundred miles to march, and our Russian winter pretty well finished them off without the help of our guerilla escorts...

So – the Moscow we knew had gone; so had young Petya, and Prince Andrei, and many thousand more. When we talk about the war, the times when, Pierre insists, "Chaos was supreme" (mark you, he was horrified by the sheer muddle and misery of the battlefield: perhaps, as a professional soldier, I can perceive an overall pattern), then Natasha, who usually bows to him completely, agreeing with all his views – she it is who will quietly remind us that God must have been somewhere, or she would not have found the wounded Andrei in time to nurse him and be reconciled with him before he died; nor Pierre freed from slavery and certain slow death with the French army at the very moment Petya was lost...

How peaceful and prosperous life is once more. Nikolai was telling us this evening how he is planning to buy back the Rostov's old country estate, bordering on Bald Hills. So the wheel comes full circle.

It was there that Prince Andrei first met Natasha,

you know. She told me once how he laughingly reminded her, at the great ball in Petersburg, how she had been in the bedroom above his, and he could hear her as she leant out of the window admiring the beauty of the moonlight, and whispering of how she felt she could fly away – and Natasha did not even know he had overheard...

And she and Nikolai were telling us about the best day's hunting they ever had there; and how they ended up at Uncle's rough old hunting lodge, and what a marvellous evening it was, with balalaika and guitar music. "And how my little sister *danced*!" cried Nikolai: "all the peasants crowded in the doorway to watch her: Russian to her very fingertips, for all her Moscow schooling, her faultless French, her ballroom *pas-de-chale* – eh, Natasha?"

And as I watched the thick-set matron, mother of four and devoted housewife – to be honest, a woman who is clearly no longer vain – I caught a glimpse in her bright eyes and sudden smile of that "little cossack" of fifteen, so impulsive and wayward, so enchanting, as I remember her standing in the middle of the gorgeous music room of the Moscow house, lifting her chin to the first few notes of the harpsichord, and pouring out her heart in my favourite barcarolle.

Above: The moonlit window through which Prince Andrei heard Natasha and fell in love with her, though it was not until after he had danced with her at the it was not until he danced with her at the Emperor's ball in St Petersburg that he asked for her hand.

Left: *Natasha's bedroom at Otradnoe. She and Sonya were trying an old charm to conjure the image of their future husbands in the looking glass. It was all in fun, but Sonya insisted she could see a face...*

P G WODEHOUSE

(1881 – 1975)

Pelham Grenville Wodehouse, the third of four brothers, was born in Guildford, Surrey, to a Hong Kong magistrate and his wife. Nicknamed "Plum", a derivative of Pelham, Wodehouse spent his infancy in Hong Kong and was then educated in England at Dulwich College where he gained considerable acclaim for his academic and sporting prowess. Deprived of a Cambridge education as a result of the decline of the Indian rupee, Wodehouse joined the Hong Kong and Shanghai Bank in London and at the same time began writing articles and short stories.

In 1901, he took a job as a journalist on *The Globe* and in 1902 his first novel, *The Potholers* was published. This was to be the first of many, and following two visits to the United States, Wodehouse took on various freelance projects. After selling some stories to *Cosmopolitan* for two hundred dollars, Wodehouse decided his luck was taking an upward turn and left *The Globe*. *Something Fresh*, the first Blandings novel, was published in the *Saturday Evening Post* in 1914 and in the same year Wodehouse met and married Ethel Rowley. He worked as a musical lyricist with Jerome Kern and Guy Bolton, and in 1920 *Piccadilly Jim* sold 200,000 copies.

Wodehouse and his wife divided their time between New York and Europe and bought houses in France and London. The first of the Wooster/Jeeves novels, *Thank You, Jeeves*, was published in 1934 and fired the opening fusillade in the Wodehouse canon. Such phrases as "I had described Roderick Spoke to the butler as a man with an eye that could open an oyster at sixty paces" have kept both sides of the Atlantic in a state of agreeable hilarity for nigh on fifty years.

In 1940, when at Le Touquet in the south of France, Wodehouse was imprisoned by the German authorities and while under house arrest agreed to make some radio programmes which he believed were to be broadcast only to the United States. Unfortunately, they were used as propaganda against the British and Wodehouse was denounced as a traitor. Although his name was later cleared, he never returned to live in England and in 1956 he and his wife became American Citizens, although retaining their British citizenship. They settled on Long Island, and in 1965 Wodehouse was clearly thrilled when the BBC made a television series based on the Wooster stories.

Wodehouse continued working until his death and in 1975 received a knighthood in the New Year's Honours List. He died on February 14 of that year, while writing *Sunset at Blandings*.

Chapter 5
BLANDINGS CASTLE

"There were times, it seemed to Gally some days after his heart to heart talk with James Piper at the Emsworth Arms, when the grounds and messuages of Blandings Castle came as near to resembling an enchanted fairytale as dammit. Strong hands had mowed the lawn till it gleamed in the sunlight, birds sang in the treetops, bees buzzed in the flowerbeds. You would not be far wrong, he thought, if you said that all Nature smiled, as he himself was doing."

(Sunset at Blandings)

"This Blessed Plot," as the downy old Bard so immortally dubbed it – and on one of his finest stints, I feel, when the sun was shining, the bees buzzing round the roses and Anne Hathaway had got the raised veal-and-ham pie just right: golden-brown and done to a turn. "This England," he went on to say, arguably to fill out the line; but he could just as well have penned "This Blandings"; and one School Of Thought, whose members meet regularly at the Pelican Club, confidently maintains that he did and then crossed it out, feeling perhaps a touch of favouritism creeping in. For Blandings Castle was flourishing in 1593; and though even the Pelican's Shakespeare-fanciers would hesitate to claim their idol Slept There, it is on the records that Queen Elizabeth did, and even Cromwell a bit later – though he was deemed to have imposed himself and certainly was never asked back.

Through the passing centuries, ever since it was set up very solidly in the mid-fifteenth or thereabouts, Blandings Castle on its knoll has dominated that stretch of Shropshire countryside, and Threepwoods have jousted, roistered, galliarded and no doubt sunk in their cups to renditions in close harmony of the more soft-centred of the latest madrigals; adding, in their leisured moments, a wing here or pulling down a turret there; Georgianising, Gothicising or Victorianising as the time and the mood took them, and ending up in the twentieth century with a spacious and comfortable dwelling of some fifty rooms, give or take the odd picture gallery, and not, of course, including the knife room, the plate room, the tack room or the flower room (the latter equipped with "bouquet bench" – part of Lady Constance's terrible bout of Americanisation as a result of marrying one) but a small price to pay for the snooker balls, heating in the lavatories and similar luxury items from that particular flurry of updating.

The most fanatical "period" stickler, the most rigid purist – even Lot's better half, the original nostalgic – would be forced to admit that, whatever else, Blandings is comfortable, indeed positively cosy, in its

modern state; and on this point I hasten to reassure nervous guests boarding the two o'clock from Paddington (the best train of the day) for the three hours and forty minutes' journey to Buildwas-for-Market-Blandings via Swindon and points west. I would go further and elaborate on the mellow evening light in the station yard gently gilding Jno Robinson's aging taxicab that has come for to carry them Castleward as smoothly as any itinerant band of angels one might spy over Jordan. Three miles meandering in a mazy motion will bring you through the great wrought-iron gates and slowly up the long, curvacious drive, with lawns and parklands prodigally laid out on either hand; then past the rhododendron shrubbery, and you will turn the last corner and see what the wooded lanes – or alternatively your total absorption in the sorting out of global problems with

Opposite: *The hall, spacious, be-galleried and be-staircased, is a place for the castle's residents, guests and impostors to idle or partake of the cup that cheers but not inebriates.*

Below: *This splendidly solid fireplace is one of the hall's finest features.*

Preceding pages: *Blandings Castle was set up very solidly in the fifteenth century or thereabouts.*
Throughout the passing years a wing may have been added here, a turret pulled down there, so that it is now a comfortable dwelling dominating its particular stretch of Shropshire countryside. This happy rendition shows the noble north-east front.

Jno Robinson – may have hidden until now: the noble north-east front of Blandings Castle.

Beach the butler will be there to greet you, and may inform you that Lady Florence – or Lady Constance, or whichever of Lord Emsworth's formidable sisters is currently making his life more complicated than necessary – is on the terrace, and that there is ample time to meet your fellow guests before changing for dinner. Beach is a remarkable man. Behind that serene, bow-fronted facade lies an obsessive hypochondriac of medal-winning complexity, involving the full gamut of feet and joints, of nervous headaches that produce a swimming sensation, a stomach-lining too sensitive even to be spoken of except at length, and the positively mediaeval tortures of the ingrowing toenail. That carefully-measured, port-ripened tone, the lowered eyelids, and the fat pale hands so patently designed for the commanding gesture – and seen in action as the under-footman takes your bags – rather than any rough or menial task: all these are monumental attributes, in the sense that, like some sacred stone which years of reverent treatment have polished to the finest of patinas, Beach is deeply smooth. He may be a martyr to the bunion and the corn, but Beach is Doing All Right.

If I appear to linger over this august personage, it is only in deference to his position. Next to the Ninth Earl himself, Beach is the most important character at

Left: The bell rack from the Butler's Pantry, domain of the inestimable Beach. Here the privileged may be invited to sample a particularly fine port.

Opposite: The billiard (or snooker) room is still a haven of gentlemanly retirement. The pleasing click of ivory upon ivory can be heard as far away as the hall.

Blandings – for those in the know. The Threepwood harpies – the Ladies Constance, Hermione, Dora, Julia and Frances (there is another, Lady Diana, but by general concensus, an absolute corker) – these sisters come and go in between or accompanied by successive husbands; but Beach is There, like Everest; unchanging as that Dorian johnnie with the heavily-curtained portrait. And with Beach as your *cicerone* and ally, all Blandings is your oyster. Moreover, along with a pet bullfinch and the treasured clipping from the Blatchford *Intelligencer and Echo* covering a tour of the Castle, his first and only mention in newsprint, Beach keeps in his Butler's Pantry a very fine old tawny, and likes to share a glass with kindred spirits. Cultivate Beach: that's about the nub of it.

It was under his aegis, though not quite the circumstances of this necessarily sketchy scenario, that I first explored Blandings. I came to the Castle, like so many a good man and true before me, as an imposter. No house party in this great Shropshire stronghold is complete without an imposter or two; and the visit I eventually pulled off – brief in blueprint but happily

extended – did in fact involve no less than three: a record, it is claimed by the experts at the Drones Club.

But how was it (I hear you ask) that Beach showed such a character round the ancestral treasures when he should more properly have been locking up the silver and breaking out the small-arms? Further light must be thrown.

Castle Blandings is generally considered one of the finest showplaces in this green and pleasant land; and the blue-chip status of Mr Beach's conducted tours has, not to put too fine a point on it, been told in Gath and published in the streets of Ashkelon; not forgetting Batchford; wherefore the charabancs of pilgrims travel from near and far: a positive caravan-serai. Orderly groups of schoolchildren, old age pensioners, choirboys, pig-fanciers and many more gather – admittedly not all at once – of a Thursday Open Day with their 2/6s to rubber-neck (as our American cousins phrase it) at the noble crenellated brow of Blandings Castle and harken to Beach's richly informative and well-round spiel.

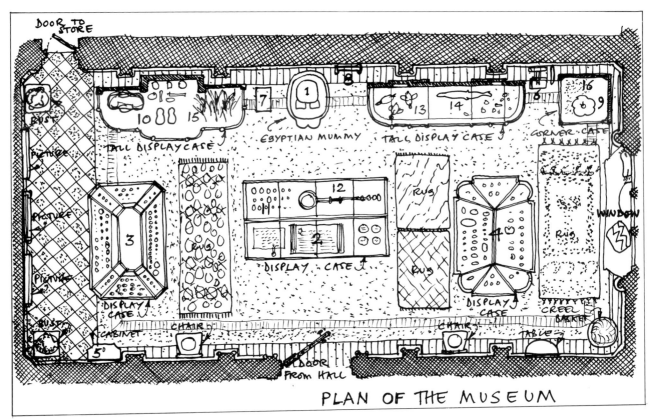

PLAN OF THE MUSEUM

I joined myself to just one such faithful band, the Sweet Afton Loyalist & Marketing Studies Society, which I discovered, on enquiry at the Shrewsbury bus depot, to be on the point of departure and, furthermore, short of the full compliment by a head. I stashed my small suitcase, standard equipment for all imposters, under my seat, and mingled. There was no great demand on my conversational skills since the assembled company struck up with a rousing Loyalist – or possibly a Marketing Studies – ditty and kept going until we halted at the Emsworth Arms in Market Blandings. Here we refreshed ourselves with the famed home brew of G. Ovens, Proprietor; and thence to Blanding Castle.

While they were gathering into a bunch in order not to miss a word of Beach's welcoming preamble, I hastily concealed my case in a rhododendron bush. I checked my moustache was in place, pulled my tasteless but effectively concealing green pork pie well down, and joined the end of the line as it was frog-marched up the small steps to the great portal – but not before I had marked, learned and inwardly digested the fact that the ivy on the East corner looked almost menacingly healthy, and reached up beyond the second floor windows.

The door opened into a spacious hall, be-galleried,

be-staircased and, on this occasion, be-red-roped and bedecked with terse notices of such uncompromising succinctness that even the thickest Wolverhampton Wanderer or Bridgnorth big-end fitter could not fail to get the message: KINDLY KEEP IN LINE, NO SMOKING, KINDLY DO NOT FINGER OBJECTS OF ART. These negative occupations seemed to concentrate the minds of the assembled sightseers wonderfully as they trouped through, glimpsing in passage the billiard-room and smoking room – the latter marginally occupied by a pair of long legs protruding from a comfortable chair and a garishly-jacketed novelette drooping from a limp hand – and so to the Museum.

The Museum at Blandings comprises an eccentric collection of objects, giving the immediate impression of a curio shop rather than a mecca for the serious student of the lesser-known Great Private Collections. Admittedly the Egyptian mummy makes an impressive start, and the Gutenberg Bible keeps up the tone; the collection of coins is passable; but thereafter it swiftly declines into a rather scruffy case of birds' eggs, a proudly displayed First World War bullet and other less glamorous implements of battle like entrenching tools and a battered mahogany thunder-box, petering out in framed certificates of adulation from the

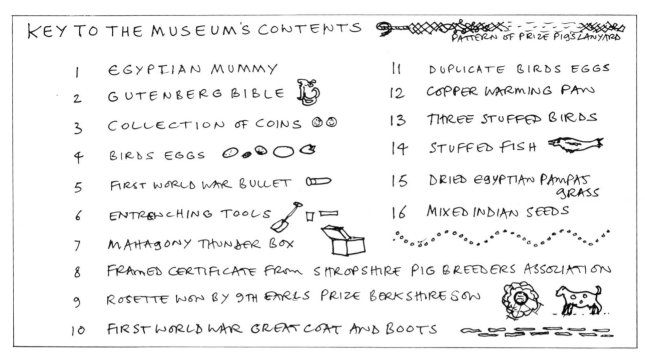

KEY TO THE MUSEUM'S CONTENTS   PATTERN OF PRIZE PIG'S LANYARD

1 EGYPTIAN MUMMY
2 GUTENBERG BIBLE
3 COLLECTION OF COINS
4 BIRDS EGGS
5 FIRST WORLD WAR BULLET
6 ENTRENCHING TOOLS
7 MAHAGONY THUNDER BOX
8 FRAMED CERTIFICATE FROM SHROPSHIRE PIG BREEDERS ASSOCIATION
9 ROSETTE WON BY 9TH EARLS PRIZE BERKSHIRE SOW
10 FIRST WORLD WAR GREAT COAT AND BOOTS

11 DUPLICATE BIRDS EGGS
12 COPPER WARMING PAN
13 THREE STUFFED BIRDS
14 STUFFED FISH
15 DRIED EGYPTIAN PAMPAS GRASS
16 MIXED INDIAN SEEDS

Shropshire Pig Breeders' Association, and even the rosette won by the 9th Earl's prize Berkshire sow. This last, however – humble as it might seem to the cursory glance – was my target.

A wager at the Drones had been the start of it; and a mere bagatelle it seemed at the time, with encouragingly generous odds laid against my success by such hardened punters as Wooster, Finknottle and even young Freddie Threepwood himself though at the moment of truth, so to speak, he would have to be away in America overseeing the interests of his dog-biscuit empire. If I removed the rosette (we decided unanimously against any or all of the three silver medals won by the sow in question, the mighty Empress of Blandings, at successive Shropshire Agricultural Shows, as being both too valuable and too close to the heart of the gentle Lord Emsworth) – if, as Browning put it, the guerdon be gained, the reward of it all, the Hon Freddie solemnly promised not only to pay up but to restore the aforesaid guerdon to the Museum, with his own hands and at the earliest opportunity. My attendance at Thursday Visitors' Day and investment of 2/6 was in the nature of a recce; and I was pleased to note, as I kept in line, refrained from smoking or fingering the objects of art – skirting meanwhile the paint-pot and brush hastily abandoned by a tall shabby odd-job man as we entered – that the rosette lay on a silver salver atop a cabinet, as distinct from being locked away inside; and a neatly printed notice demonstrated this was indeed my prize. No

question, need I say, of pocketing it then and there: that would have been tantamount to "fingering a work of art", even in the broadest-minded of interpretations. Enough for me that I had the prey in my sights.

One version of the plan was to wander down to the pigsty – or even further afield – and be abandoned as lost by the charabanc party; then change into evening dress (the suitcase in the shrubbery), mingle with the guests before dinner claiming I was an old friend of Freddie's and hadn't he mentioned I would be dropping in on my way to an Old Boy's gathering at my Shropshire prep school? – drift into the Museum, pocket the rosette and depart after a suitably gracious farewell. Imagine my discomfiture, therefore, when all at once the lanky figure of Buffy Desnoes emerged, cue in hand and a far-away look in his eye as though wondering when and where tea, or even something stronger, would be on the cards. Buffy is none other than my brother-in-law: a splendid fellow if none too quick of brain; it was only his preoccupation with the next round of refreshments that saved me that day – though the green pork pie may have added a touch of verisimilitude to an otherwise bald and unconvincing incognito, as W.S.Gilbert would have phrased it. Fearing that any moment Buffy might whoop out some clan greeting-call and blow my cover, I shuffled closer into the shadow of the amazon-wife of a Sweet Afton Marketing Studies expert (or Loyalist); and Beach's rounded phrases led us away from the danger spot, up the grand staircase and along the gallery to goggle at the Library, the Amber Drawing Room, the tapestries and the family portraits. "Please, Mr Beach, might I enquire if the nobility actually use the rooms?" the amazon asked. "Certainly, madam: his Lordship and guests are wont to gather in this very salon before dining." Aha! thought I; and then, Blow! For how could I gather with them if old Bluffy, who knows all about the wager – indeed bet against my success – was going to haloo, "Oh, so you're having a go, are you, old fruit?" Plan two would have to be employed: the surreptitious rather than the blatant entry. Up the ivy after lights-out.

It did not prove difficult to break away from the main party at the point where Beach led them through the green baize door to the working part of the Castle, murmuring something to the effect that the old kitchen had been virtually unchanged since the sixteenth century and adding that there might be refreshments in the servants' hall if Mrs Twemlow could accomodate the numbers. Reducing those numbers by one, I slipped out of a side door and encountered again the tramp-like odd-job man from the Museum. He wore a patched and sagging jacket, an ancient, wilting fishermans' hat, and said "Eh?" with the manner of a startled fawn when I asked him the way to the pig-sty. On my repeating the question he brightened visibly. "Capital. Capital," he said. "Capital! You're fond of pigs too then?"

Feeling immediately involved by this assumption, I nodded, and he led me through the kitchen garden and across a small paddock, all buttercups and daisies like the legendary path to Strawberry Fair; and as we sauntered he told me how he hoped this chappie who was staying might agree to paint a portrait of his prize pig, the Empress of Blandings: an invitation turned down, he pointed out with some disgust, by many a Royal Academician in his time. After a brief digression on his favourite reading, Whipple's *On the Care of the Pig*, he returned to the subject of the projected painting. "I intend to hang it in the portrait gallery, along with the ancestors. My sisters keep objecting, you see, even when I point out that anything would be an improvement on the likeness of my maternal grandmother – you may have noticed her in the hall, by the by: some misguided notion that portraying her as Venus rising from the sea might divert the eye from her indubitable similarity to George Robey...'

So this was Lord Emsworth, the 9th Earl himself.

Proudly he led me over to the palatial brick-and-timber sty and, in response to his "chirrup", as he called it, a rising call of "Pig-Hoo-Ey!", the Empress emerged: the most enormous pig I have ever seen – not that I would set myself up as an expert in this field. Lord Emsworth gazed adoringly at her and, like some obscure litanist, started to recite her diet: "Daily nourishment amounting to fifty-seven hundred calories, these to consist of protein four pounds five ounces, carbohydrates twenty-five pounds..." and so on. "I do hope," he added, "that the portrait will do her justice. Unfortunately Beach the butler seems to have the idea that this nice young man who is about to start on it is some sort of an imposter..."

The plot thickens; indeed, is in danger of positively curdling. I had time to ponder on this when – the Earl having been summoned to the telephone – I concealed myself in a potting shed and waited for the sound of the departing charabanc. I may have nodded off with the warmth of the day and the humidity of the manure sacks behind which I sheltered in the arms of a deck-chair not in its first bloom of youth. I was awakened by the shed door's gentle opening and sounds of furtive movements on the far side of my richly scented screen. Lying low, I was able to observe, through a convenient cranny, a small wiry man of the sort variously described as "a shifty little tyke", "bad news" and "clearly up to no good"; he was engaged in the act of changing his tyke-ish gear for the footman's uniform he produced from the obligatory small suitcase.

Could this be yet another imposter? I asked myself (as the French have a way of putting it) – for clearly he would be woefully miscast as the guest/artist imposter of whom Lord Emsworth had expressed such fond hopes. The plot now showed signs of solidifying out of all recognition. Personally, however, I was in no position either to confront this new ingredient on the spot, and even less to march up to the Castle a few paces in the rear and unmask him. No: I must bide my time. When the psuedo-footman had exited as furtively as he had entered, I opened my sandwiches and prepared to wait for nightfall.

I retrieved my suitcase after dark and changed into evening dress, in the possibly fond and foolish trust that whatever *dénouement* might ensue, I would be treated with more suitable respect if so attired and, moreover, less ripely redolent of my chosen hiding place. Approaching Blandings Castle at night is almost as impressive as the daytime encounter, as one

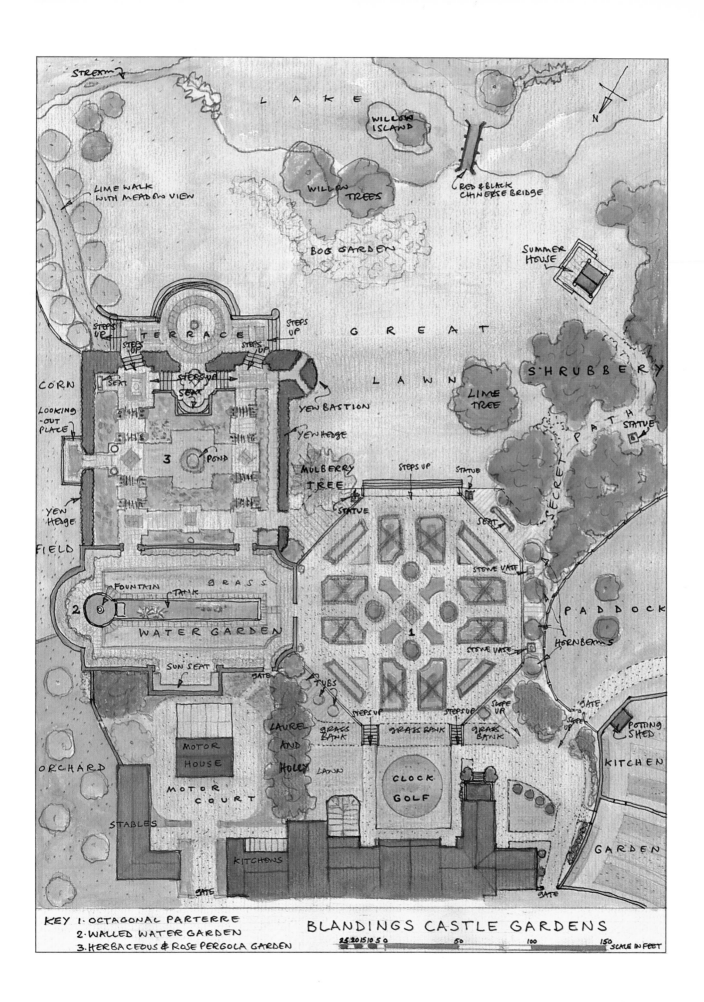

STREAM

L A K E

WILLOW ISLAND

WILLOW TREES

RED & BLACK CHINESE BRIDGE

N

LIME WALK WITH MEADOW VIEW

BOG GARDEN

SUMMER HOUSE

TERRACE

STEPS UP

STEPS UP

STEPS UP

STEPS UP

STEPS UP

SEAT

SEAT

G R E A T

L A W N

S H R U B B E R Y

CORN

LOOKING -OUT PLACE

3

POND

YEW BASTION

YEW HEDGE

MULBERRY TREE

LIME TREE

STEPS UP

STATUE

SECRET PATH

STATUE

STATUE

YEW HEDGE

SEAT

FIELD

FOUNTAIN

TANK

G R A S S

STONE VASE

2

WATER GARDEN

1

P A D D O C K

SUN SEAT

GATE

TUBS

STEPS UP

STONE VASE

HORNBEAMS

LAUREL AND HOLLY

GRASS BANK

GRASS BANK

STEPS UP

GRASS BANK

SLOPE UP

GATE

SLOPE UP

ORCHARD

MOTOR HOUSE

LAWN

POTTING SHED

MOTOR COURT

CLOCK GOLF

KITCHEN

STABLES

GARDEN

KITCHENS

GATE

GATE

KEY 1·OCTAGONAL PARTERRE
2·WALLED WATER GARDEN
3·HERBACEOUS & ROSE PERGOLA GARDEN

BLANDINGS CASTLE GARDENS

25 20 15 10 5 0   50   100   150
SCALE IN FEET

rounds the shrubbery on the blaze of lights from scores of windows, spilling over the terraces and lawns. High above against the moonwashed sky, the battlements loom like a mountain, and farther away, touched by that same moon, the dark cedars, the distant lake and its Grecian temple. Slowed but not halted by this stunning nocturnal scene, I made my way across the terrace and peered cautiously through the dining room window. Sure enough, there was Lord E., two fine gorgon-sisters, a niece or two, old Buffy Desnoes tucking into the *bombe surprise*, and a nice-looking cove with an unconventionally floppy velvet tie: the artist-imposter, I assumed, and acting more attentive than strictly necessary to the prettiest niece-figure. One of the footmen serving at table, moreover, was none other than the furtive tyke.

Oh for a tongue of fire, or preferably several – a pentecostal outbreak of same – to describe the scene when at last, in the witching hour after midnight, I was occupied in climbing up the ivy to gain access by an open bedroom window and, glancing sideways, observed the tyke shinning up a garden ladder not forty feet away, but too full of his evil intent to notice yours truly flattened among the luxuriant foliage. So now it was a race: there was clearly more at stake than the Empress's rosette. I hastened to infenestrate the chosen bedroom, fell loudly over a collection of jugs, shoe-trees and other highly collectable ephemera clearly arranged to alert the nervous sleeper of just such an intrusion, and picked myself up to discover no sleeper present: the invitingly turned-down bed had not even been used. By the palettes and easel employed in the barricade, I surmised it to be the artist-imposter's room; but there was no time for idle speculation: the tyke might already be about whatever nefarious night-work such characters get up to.

I was out in the corridor and running down the main staircase before I realised there was a Watcher in the gallery. It leapt from its enshrouding blankets waving a pocket torch: an apparition not for a moment to be mistaken for the White Lady of Blandings whose head was chopped off by her husband back in the Middle Ages and now does the rounds, they do say, with it tucked possessively under one arm... It was at the bottom of the staircase that the long-anticipated *dénouement* attained full ripeness, as, in a gloom relieved only by a shakily-aimed pencil-beam, the artist-imposter, the footman-ditto, myself and the lone watcher (the Earl's over-efficient secretary, clearly primed for just such a melodrama) collided with each other, a small occasional table of china ornaments and a suit of armour.

There were shouts, a mass opening of bedroom doors; and only our interlocked and prone position saved us four from the volley of Beach's grapeshot and the bigger battalions of Lord Emsworth's revolver. Lights came on, bodies were sorted and helped to their several feet. Beach telephoned for the police while I and the artist relieved the tyke of Lady Hermione's garnets, and held him fast in our own version of the classic half Nelson. The wretched secretary retired to have his bruises salved; while Lord Emsworth took us – me and the artist chappie: a frightfully good sort, who turned out, as your friendly narrator had suspected all along, to be the penniless true love of the prettiest niece recently incarcerated at Blandings on account of her misplaced passion – Lord E. swept us, as I was saying, into the Library for a reviving noggin.

It was a time of thanks, a time for confessions. The 9th Earl insisted on presenting the aspiring lover with a handsome advance payment on the Empress's portrait to facilitate elopement; and readily loaned me the precious rosette, in grateful recognition of services rendered. After all, the wager had simply stipulated I should lay hands on the Museum's noblest treasure by fair means or foul, and produce it at the Drones Club as proof. Not even Buffy Desnoes would ever twig, Lord Emsworth assured me, topping up my glass; at which point Beach, still clad in a magnificent dressing-gown that, if anything, enhanced his imperial mien, drifted in with a cold collation to fill the space beneath the cummerbund where by rights a dinner should have lain.

FRANZ KAFKA

(1883 – 1924)

Franz Kafka was born in Prague, Czechoslovakia, the son of an Austrian-Jewish shopkeeper. His two elder brothers died before he was five years old and though he had three younger sisters and lived at home, he remained detatched from much of his family. He had very little in common with his father, finding him boorish in manner and overwhelming in build, and this caused the young Kafka to become even more insular and self absorbed.

In 1901 he enrolled at the Deutsche Universitat to read Chemistry but rapidly switched to Law, while following other courses in German Literature and the History of Art. After his final exams he worked in a law firm and wrote in his spare time. He also kept a detailed and vivid diary of his thoughts and experiences. A sickly youth, often suffering from sleeplessness and headaches, he had to take constant "reviving" holidays, interspersed with visits to a sanitarium. In 1915, he got engaged to Felice Bauer, a girl he had met little, but with whom he shared a prolific correspondence. Having joined an insurance firm, he travelled occasionally to Vienna, Venice and Verona and became passionately involved with Zionism.

Kafka wrote continually, though his depression often hindered his creativity, and it is interesting to note that the word "Schloss" in German can mean both "key" and "lock" – both signifying isolation and contriction, prevalent themes in *The Castle*.

In August 1917 Kafka started spitting blood and tuberculosis was diagnosed. Despite his worsening illness, he began a relationship with Dora Dymant, aged nineteen, which lasted until his death in June 1924. *The Castle*, his final, unfinished novel, first appeared in print in 1926.

Chapter 6

THE CASTLE

"On the whole this distant prospect of the Castle satisfied K.'s expectations. It was neither an old stronghold nor a new mansion, but a rambling pile consisting of innumerable small buildings closely packed together and of one or two storeys; if K. had not known that it was a castle he might have taken it for a little town. There was only one tower as far as he could see, whether it belonged to a dwelling house or a church he could not determine. Swarms of crows were circling round it."

W hat is your business at the Castle, then?" the landlord asked. "Why are you so anxious to get there? And you certainly seem to be anxious, if you'll pardon the observation: we all saw the way you came in and looked around; yes, and your eyeing the peasants so suspiciously when they turned round their chairs to watch you. What right have you to survey them like that, with that haughty dismissive look? It appeared haughty and dismissive to me; and my wife said the same. She saw you come in and heard you asking for a bed; and she considers your tone was far too peremptory; and, in her opinion, the claim that you were 'tired from travelling' was no excuse. Then you walk across as though you owned the place – eyeing the perfectly reputable regulars here (and each one with names and papers in order, I can assure you), while all they did was arrange themselves in a circle so they could all see you properly and watch just what you were getting up to. And you march up to the stove and warm your hands, as though for all the world you were some minor official taking pride of place.

"You *are* a sort of official, you say? Now wait: you are not from the Castle but you are here on official work for them, by arrangement? And what do you have to prove that? Oh come now: you must have papers... A letter from the Count himself? What do you take us for, pray? The Count has no need to set pen to paper, with all his administrative departments working day and night to protect him from such petty business matters, and to keep everything running smoothly. Here, it's not even properly signed; 'p.p.' – not an abbreviation they often use: far too easy to forge. No, you have to have some official papers. Wait a minute, please: one of the messengers is drinking in the inner room. He will telephone the Castle, I expect, if he's not retired yet, and find out if anyone there knows about you...

"Well, sir, apparently he managed to contact the relevant department, but the assistant to the Superintendent's clerk in charge of such enquiries was not available; and yes, indeed you will have to wait, while the correct documentation is pinpointed, the official order given and the process set in motion whereby a letter will be sent down and delivered by one of the messengers to confirm your precise status and rights. Meanwhile, he suggests I give you the room at the top of the house. It will be just a

Left: The inn where the traveller finds cold comfort, and the eyes of the villagers upon him.

Following pages: *The Castle – more a collection of smaller buildings – dominates the landscape and the lives around it.*

temporary arrangement while your position is sorted out and made absolutely clear. That's it: first the letter; and then you will have to be interviewed by one of the Castle officials: probably the under-secretary to the assistant of the Director of Internal Affairs, whose department it is, I expect – or it could be Department X. And maybe you will actually be called before the assistant himself, if you are prepared to wait your turn: he does come down every so often to the other inn – the Herrenhof. That is where the Castle personnel hold their inquiries, and sometimes even stay overnight, if the paperwork cannot be satisfactorily concluded in the time allotted: a tiring and meticulous business, you understand, dealing with all the relevant forms, memoranda, notices of deferral and letters of recommendation – and, with a lot of them, in due course, the vital counterfoils or, alternatively, the blue slips, for filing; and then the others – duplicates, apart from the official stamp of course – for the messengers to keep: they're in sole charge of tho e, naturally. Quite a responsibility; no wonder the post of messenger is so sought after: a great privilege, and a post of enormous weight and respect; not only their part of the paperwork – the end of the chain, so to speak – but in their exhausting and very demanding role as the only regular liaison between the Castle itself and the village. So, whoever you turn out to be, I strongly advise you to treat them with due deference. You can always tell a messenger by his distinguishing dress: the tight-fitting garments – very smart; not the sort of clothes a field worker or an artisan could be doing with. You will see even at some distance, and realise: This is a messenger from the Castle. And you do appreciate, I trust, that these are men who actually walk along the great corridors up there, and wait in the offices, or just outside, until they are needed; and they see the officials passing in and out, and even to speak to. Not that they tell tales, of course; but you can't help hearing them talking among themselves sometimes of these matters – and even of the great names themselves: of Herr Klamm, the chief of Department X; or Sordini in Department B, so highly reputed for his conscientiousness and scrupulous attention to detail – a true master of the memorandum, they say. Then there is the Castellan, and the Under-Castellans; Herr Fritz is one of those, I

believe, and can be very useful, if not actually influential. And there's Herr Momus: you might well be interviewed by him in person, at the Herrenhof. They have electric light there, you know; and it is all very well set up and comfortable, with countless rooms of varying and indeterminate size where they can hold their interviews and inquiries, and retire to bed when they need to, and possibly continue next day. The most important of them? Well, I do know – but it's no good your getting impatient, you must realise: I doubt if you could see *him*... It's Herr Klamm: he is certainly the most powerful and important of the Castle officials who actually come down here. He sits in the inner room at the Herrenhof, and only Frieda looks after him: the barmaid there. She is his current mistress, you understand, which makes her a very influential person. Ah: I can see you're interested right away! Certainly women play quite a part in dealings with the Castle up there: my own wife has been honoured; and, though that was some years ago, you can still tell by her bearing that she has, so to speak, moved in the company of the great. Oh yes: a beautiful woman, and in the right place at the right moment, can do very well for herself – not to mention her family and friends. But then there is a young woman in the village, Amalia, who was foolish enough to – you won't believe this, but it's true – to tear up! Yes, *tear up* a letter from Sortini himself – No: Sortini, not Sordini; just which his department is, I couldn't say: but he is clearly very powerful; and it was he who came down from the Castle in person to officiate at the handing over of the new fire engine. Well, this Amalia caught his eye: she was dressed up in all her finery that day – her father was involved in the ceremony, you see: something to do with the manning side of the fire department, I believe. But the point is, Sortini was actually observed to make a slight movement towards her. Then, later on, he sent a messenger to her with a letter: an actual letter in his own hand – and she simply went and tore it up into little pieces! Well, as you can imagine, it was the end of her and her entire family. No one speaks to them now; and her brother Barnabas – such a fine-looking young man, a hard worker and full of promise as an aspiring messenger – he suffered terribly as a result: still hangs about up there in the minor

Left: *The Castle itself is composed of numerous structures, the tallest of which is the tower, pierced by meagre windows and circled by crows.*

corridors in case someone may give him a message, from crack of dawn, and all dressed up in the tight-fitting suit his sisters made for him – but not official, not quite right, you see. There's no more employing any member of her family: neighbours took back the shoes they'd brought in for mending, and the pieces of dress-making the girls were working on. The father used to wait by the roadside where the Castle carriages drive by, hoping to speak to one of the officials: waiting and waiting. Well, he's a broken man now...

"The road to the Castle? Oh, you did look for a road, did you? Perhaps you thought you could just go up there and ring the bell? Tried to get there by road: that's a good one! Well, it's certainly odd – since you put it like that – how, whichever way you follow, you never seem to get any closer: it turns this way and that, but never towards the Castle itself. Well, it's not for the likes of us... Me, I couldn't rightly say what goes on up there in those departments. Someone told me that the messengers are admitted into certain rooms; but that there are barriers which no one actually tells you not to cross – and you are watched all the time up at the Castle. Or so we think. I was told of a great room – not Klamm's, nor even the bureau of anything in particular – that is divided in two by a desk that stretched from wall to wall the full length, where these huge books lie open; and the officials read them. The clerks sit at low tables in front of the desk to take dictation, which is always given in a whisper. Sometimes Klamm comes in. It's hard to describe him, they say: he looks different, depending on which messenger he's speaking to, whether he's up at the Castle, or down at the Herrenhof – so that it's hard even to know whether it's really him. All we can be sure of is that officials like that, and Sordini, and Sortini, and Momus, can make or break us all with the stroke of a pen, or destroy us simply with the waiting and hoping in cold corridors or out in the inn yard in all weathers, hour after hour, day after day. So all I can say to you is that you'd better get some sort of recognition from the Castle soon. And you can't just hang around here either; if you're not officially anyone, then you're a stranger; and hospitality is not a custom here. What should we want with visitors? There, see? It's light now – so you won't be needing the room."

Outside, quite suddenly, another day had begun; someone up there had switched it on. People got up and started moving again, stiffly and purposefully, each about his own business.

THOMAS MANN

(1875 – 1955)

Thomas Mann was born in the pretty North German riverside town of Lübeck, the second son of a prosperous merchant and, with his five brothers and sisters, was educated privately. His father was Mayor of the city as well as heading the ancestral firm and in 1884, Thomas was persuaded to become an apprentice to an insurance company in Munich. However, he soon tired of this and enrolled at Munich University as an auditor.

He began writing and editing articles for local journals and in 1895 travelled to Rome to join his elder brother, Heinrich. Mann then spent some time in Italy, gaining friends and experience before returning to Munich where he took up writing full time. While working on *Buddenbrooks* in 1898, Mann visited his native town of Lübeck, and then went on to Copenhagen. The book was completed in 1900, after which he took up a short period of military service.

In 1905 he Mann married the young and intelligent Katia Pringsheim, and continued to lecture and write. He was awarded the 1929 Nobel Prize for Literature and in 1933 he and his Family left Germany for Switzerland and the United States. They returned to Switzerland in 1952 where Mann produced his final novel, *The Confessions of Felix Krull, Confidence Man*. He died there in 1955.

Chapter 7

BUDDENBROOKS

"Consul Buddenbrook stood with his hands in his trousers pockets and listened to their footsteps as they died away down the empty, damp, dimly lighted street. He shivered a little in his light clothes as he stood there a few paces from his own house, and turned to look up at its grey gabled facade. His eyes lingered upon the motto carved in stone over the entrance, in antique lettering; Dominus providebit *– 'The Lord will provide.' He bowed his head a little and went in, bolting the door carefully behind him. Then he locked the vestibule door and walked slowly across the echoing floor of the great entry."*

90

I am Christian Buddenbrook, the black sheep of the family. I pride myself on always having been a detached observer – too detached, Thomas would say: but maybe I alone can see the Fall of the House of Buddenbrook clearly enough to chart its decline, from the highest social and civic status in a great merchant town, to its virtual annihilation – and all within a mere half-century. Now only my sister Tony and myself survive that fifty years, poor remnants of a mighty line; she still lives on in Lübeck, I believe, quietly fading in straightened circumstances, with her daughter and granddaughter. I wonder how they manage.

But Antonie Buddenbrook was always a survivor, with a marvellously childish sense of her own importance: in spite of two marriages and two divorces, she has never really grown up; and although her passion has always been houses and their elaborate furnishing, she adapts each time, absorbed in feathering each smaller and smaller nest... Marvellously unaware, too, of how others really see her, and see through her: I find I almost envy her the satisfaction and self-fulfilment she seemed to enjoy on every great occasion, even Father's funeral – good God: even Tom's – as though she were still centre stage, the little queen she always fancied herself. Both she and Thomas, my elder brother (very much Head of the Family), had this fanatical devotion to The Name, The Firm, The Prestige. Ironical, how vociferously they decried my love for the theatre; and yet they spent their whole lives playing these self-appointed roles, so frightfully aware of their "position", while I capered round the perimeter of the sawdust ring making people laugh.

Tom, in fact - always concerned with elegance – became obsessive about his clothes and toilette in middle age: even when things were going badly for the firm, he continued to have his suits made in Hamburg by the best tailors; and Herr Wenzel the barber came to the house every morning – such pomading of hair, such curling and waxing of moustaches! By the end he was just another frightened actor hiding behind an imposing *maquillage*.

Or so I think. Tom and I quarrelled very bitterly in the later years. I especially remember the scene just after Mother's death, when I admitted my intention – now that Mamma could not be upset – of marrying my longtime love in Hamburg. "All I want is a home," I said, "and sympathetic company for my old age: we're both rather damaged goods—" But Tom was furious. "How do you know the child is yours, you simple fool? And her other children? I suppose they and this bastard between them are to enjoy your quarter of the family inheritance? Well, I shall put a stop to *that*." And he could: the will had made him guardian of my affairs – after some little irregularities and misfortunes on my part – and he would see to it I had only a monthly allowance in the future.

So that was when it all came out. I could not help it: I had restrained my resentment too long. I railed against his smug position in life, his precious Equilibrium; all the tact and propriety: he was an ice-cold egotist, I said, who withdrew into his elegant, remote little soul if anyone tried to justify *their* way— And suddenly he seemed to shrink. He looked

Left: *Christmas in the dining room of the Buddenbrook family's Lübeck mansion. The lily-spangled tree reaches almost to the ceiling and the air is heavy with the smell of fir needles and gingerbread. From the kitchen* (right) *comes the clattering of pans and the smell of onions frying.*

unhealthy, and terribly weary. He said: "But I'm only like this because I have always been afraid of becoming like you..."

Well, he put a stop to my hopes, just as he said he would: Property and the Family Name, his twin gods, his equilibrium, were at risk.

This very concrete abstract – Property – is perhaps the villain of the piece: if I were writing a play, instead of these rambling jottings, I would have to bring this out. I suppose I would open with the House-warming at the great family mansion in Meng Street, symbol of the Buddenbrook fortunes at their height, and crowd it with all the relations and the powerful burghers of Lübeck. I might have the curtain rise on a painted drop, brilliantly lit with late afternoon sun, of the front of the huge house – the plaque over the portal: *Dominus Providebit*, God will provide (no doubts there!). I'd bring up the lights inside, in the Landscape Room, and raise the drop as the assembled company started talking... Talking about the family that had built it in 1682 and flourished and fallen so

suddenly, it seemed, on hard times (the suspect partner, of course, and the Napoleonic wars), making it possible for the up-and-coming Buddenbrooks (established 1768 – but starting long before with that "well-to-do tailor" of Rostock so lovingly recorded in the annals) to get it at a good price – "*Assez!*" the imposing grandfather figure would say, and delicately turn the subject, as though he sensed the ironical future in another's fragile greatness... And I would bring in the children as light relief: the eldest, barely ten and already quietly responsible; the little princess Antonie, acutely aware of just how much a mop of golden curls and a roguish manner will get her; and the clown-brother, the odd-looking one, making the most of the only remaining role – and the whole well-dressed, well-fed company laughs heartily.

What a stage set, though! That long Landscape Room on the first floor, named for its tapestries; and the dining room (here the tapestries are vaguely classical, with statued gods and goddesses); and the great pillared hall outside: not only grandeur and conspicuous possessions, but the cosiness, the security and – oh yes – the true warmth running deep, under all the gossip and good manners and observance of tradition. Not the least of these traditions, mark you, is Restraint: it is unseemly, unconventional, to show your emotions, or talk about your doubts, worries, illnesses, even with your nearest and dearest – much less with Consul Kröger, Pastor Wunderlich, Herr Gratjens the Broker or Herr Köppen the Wine Merchant. It's the price of grain, the election of a new Senator, mergers and betrothals: these are acceptable subjects; this is a society, a circle, in which one soon learns that possessions count for more than individuals. Perhaps there are no individuals, even in that colourful crowd at the house-warming: only representatives of clans, or firms, or institutions. And they are all dwarfed by the stage set, the Meng Street house, symbol of the success they all spend their lives creating and preserving.

So – fill it with more occasions, and a crowd of extras, stage-hands in fustian. Let us have weddings and christenings and betrothals in quick succession, like a slide show. And the great Christmas party, all the old rituals observed: the choristers assemble in the pillared hall; the glass doors are open into the Landscape Room where family and friends are gathered; the carols, the readings, the prayers, and at last *Tannenbaum*, as the white folding doors into the dining room are opened and the company troops

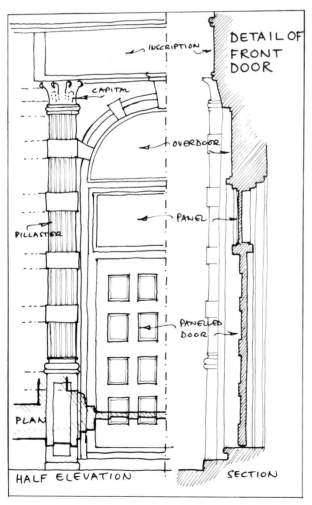

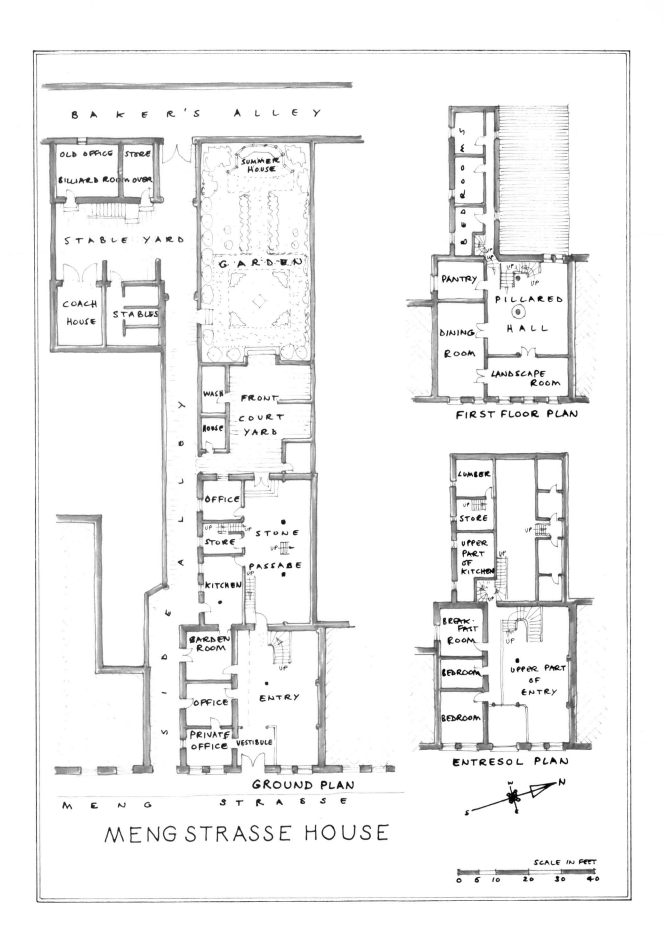

BAKER'S ALLEY

OLD OFFICE STORE
BILLIARD ROOM OVER

STABLE YARD

COACH HOUSE   STABLES

SUMMER HOUSE

GARDEN

WASH HOUSE   FRONT COURT YARD

OFFICE
STORE   STONE
UP   PASSAGE
KITCHEN
GARDEN ROOM

OFFICE   ENTRY

PRIVATE OFFICE   VESTIBULE

GROUND PLAN

MENG   STRASSE

PANTRY
PILLARED HALL

DINING ROOM
LANDSCAPE ROOM

FIRST FLOOR PLAN

LUMBER
STORE
UPPER PART OF KITCHEN
BREAK-FAST ROOM
BEDROOM   UPPER PART OF ENTRY
BEDROOM

ENTRESOL PLAN

MENG STRASSE HOUSE

SCALE IN FEET
0 5 10   20   30   40

93

slowly in to – Paradise! Suddenly, after sombre reverence and *Silent Night*, a positive explosion of light and noise: cries of wonder and excitement, and every candle and gas jet lit in the overflowing treasure-cave. The long table is piled with presents, and smaller piles for dependents near the door. The tree reaches up to the ceiling, spangled with white lilies; and the very air is heavy with the smell of hot fir needles and gingerbread, wafting out to those servants and members of the deserving poor who wait in the passage, and now come forward to receive their knitted comforters and serviceable shoes. Soon the family and guests are exclaiming over their own and others' gifts: objects of porcelain, gold, silver and silk in abundance, and the marvellous toy theatre or long-awaited hobby-horse for the children. Meanwhile, great platters of gingerbreads and sweetmeats and bowls of almond cream are consumed, and the maids move with tea and biscuits through the happy throng. Later, of course, comes The Dinner, for which the older children stay – but as soon as I was an adult I would slip off to the club in the interim, getting back in time or a little late for the meal itself, which was held by tradition in the columned hall outside.

The hall was used for all important functions where large numbers were involved. In my play I would have a wedding there, I think, or maybe a funeral, with the deceased Buddenbrook in a handsome coffin laid out on a long table for the cream of Lübeck to pay its last respects. (There was a sofa encircling the central pillar, to which I retired after the house-warming, I remember – I must have been seven – saying "I'm ill, Mamma, damned ill!": enjoying the effect of my new word. And old Doctor Grabow recommending – always, whatever the complaint – "a little pigeon, a little French bread.") Stage right, the white carved wooden staircase leads up to the second storey where we and our parents slept; stage left, a corridor of rooms used for guests. Below, in my brightly-lighted dollshouse, you would see the *entresol* off the big landing, containing the breakfast room and my grandparents' apartments overlooking the garden; and in spite of the number and complexity of rooms, there is an airy spaciousness largely due, of course, to the great entry hall, two storeys high – then the offices on the ground floor and out at the back, along the broad stone passage past the kitchen and the servants' quarters. Then the glass door to the courtyards, stables and finally the annexe, with the billiard-room upstairs, some humbler bedrooms, and storerooms

galore: a big, rambling house. We all took it so much for granted, like the safe spot you mark off when playing War, to run to and rest there: no one could touch you till you left it...

Where would I bring down the *entrácte* curtain, I wonder? At some point just past the tilt of the mighty Equilibrium? A happy climax, perhaps, for the Old Firm, as represented by Thomas Buddenbrook— But there were so many triumphs: his brilliant marriage, the christening of the much-needed son and heir, the election to Senator, the building of the splendid new house (so very like the old: so significant in its denial of innovation; safely choosing to ape past grandeur). And then the Hundredth Anniversary of the Firm: yes, that is the bittersweet moment I would choose.

A couple of months before, Thomas Buddenbrook had accepted his first and, I think, only shady deal. Tony could not resist telling me of it _ in deepest confidence – as she had been responsible: the husband of an aristocratic friend needed the money fast, and offered his grain harvest for sale "in the blade" to raise it. "I had a hard time budging him," she said, glowing with the new-found importance of "business acumen", as she put it: "I pointed out he wasn't having the success he once did because he was far too cautious and conscientious, letting slip the chances for a *coup* – like this one." Now there is a wise old saw inscribed in the Family Book: "My son, attend with zeal to thy business by day; but do none that hinders thee from thy sleep by night." Moreover, Tom's first clash with me, the occasion of my leaving the firm, had been over a careless remark of mine at the club, a joke, which he translated freely as "All business men are swindlers." Like his forbears, he was fanatical about the firm's honoured Name – all the more so as he lacked their solid Lutheran faith in the triumph of the Good; and, in changing times, saw all around him rivals who zealously attended to increasing their business by any means and still slept soundly at night. So I knew what an inner struggle must have ensued before he accepted the "challenge" and bought that harvest in the blade.

So – our *entrácte* curtain: the Hundredth Anniversary of Buddenbrooks; a brilliant day in July, flags out

Opposite: The landscape room on the first floor, named for its tapestries. It is here that the family sit to catch the sun and where friends and business associates gather to celebrate weddings, christenings and betrothals, smug in the observance of unchanging ritual.

Following pages: *The family's great Meng Street mansion, symbol of the Buddenbrook fortunes at their height. While the family declined the house survived, and now, as louder music and coarser laughter echo through its halls, the place positively flourishes.*

Left: *Through the pillared and flagstoned hall you can see the office* (right). *Behind the glass double doors is the hub of the Buddenbrook business empire.*

all over town; the grand new house (use the old set with some pompous white caryatids planted on the front), crowded inside and out with family, friends, business colleagues and rivals, employees, tradesmen *et al* – even a band playing "Now thank we all our God" and bits of Offenbach. But why does the man of the moment seem so absent and preoccupied? Why does he stand there by the window watching the clouds roll up (bring down the lights slowly: a nice effect). Why his shocked reaction to that sudden patter on the glass, for all the world as though it were grapeshot instead of mid-summer hail? The festivities swirl round him, the music loud and tinny as the inevitable telegram is carried to him through the throng. Now the sun is shining again; but that harvest, his shady *coup*, is flat on its face.

It is a ripe moment, the effect only heightened by the protagonist's immaculate behaviour: his elegant façade collapses only with his sudden death – and the Meng Street house survives even the final curtain: for the theme of the tragedy, the true irony, is the sacrifice of people on the altar of Propriety. I can see now that Tony was forced against her will into her first disastrous marriage, to a husband who, as later emerged, had only propped his failing business on the strength of his betrothal to a Buddenbrook; and her second marriage she needed desperately for her own

sense of importance: it was no holiday being a divorced dependent in her mother's increasingly pious household. And Thomas encouraged her: it seemed the safe and respectable way out. Both Tony and I were an embarrassment: stumbling-blocks to his ambitions, extra worries for a worried man as the business slid downhill, and no doubt contributing to his early death. So many died: Tom, and Clara – the youngest of the four of us – and even little Johann, the last of the line. As old Sesemi Weichbrodt would pronounce, standing on tiptoe – so tiny, so fragile and hump-backed, yet fettered by relentlessly good health to this sinful world – "It is not right!"; to which I with my delicate constitution (you see, all my nerves are too short the whole way down this side), would simply add: "It is not *fair!*"

As I say, the house remains. Nowadays, louder music and coarser laughter ring through its halls: a new up-and-coming clan is in residence – the Hagenströms. They have always been the natural rivals of the Buddenbrooks: *nouveau riche*, utterly scorned by Tony; contending with Thomas in the council, and spawning a brood of big blond boys who used to bully little Johann at school. There has been conspicuous spending of money, and the house in Meng Street positively flourishes. This thing Property is more fickle than any woman.

GIUSEPPE DI LAMPEDUSA

(1896 – 1957)

Giuseppe di Lampedusa was born a Sicilian prince in 1896. His only novel, *The Leopard*, was published posthumously, as was hailed by the French poet, Aragon, as "One of the great books of the century, one of the great books of always".

Di Lampedusa's family, the Tomasi, can be traced back to Tiberius I, Emperor of Byzantium in the sixth century. Later, a branch settled in Sicily, and in the eighteenth century one prince married a lady of German descent. They had a son, Don Giulio Maria Fabrizio, a distinguished mathematician and astronomer who received a prize at the Sorbonne in 1885. It is from this history that di Lampedusa created the characters in his novel.

As a young man, he was estranged from his father and his mother closed the family home and left Palermo to travel, following a scandal involving the murder of her sister by a lover in 1911. Di Lampedusa became a regular officer of the artillery and served on the Balkan Front during the First World War. He was taken prisoner but escaped, crossing Europe in disguise and on foot. He left regular service in 1945 but did not marry until he was thirty-four, meeting his wife, Alessandre von Wolfe Stomersee, at the Italian Embassy in London. She became an eminent Freudian analyst and like her husband spoke five languages, the two of them often reading to one another from Flaubert, Forster, Tolstoy and Dickens.

Di Lampedusa had a deep love of books and travel and, encouraged by his wife, decided to write his recollections of the family palace in Palermo, which had been destroyed in 1943. He noted such eccentricities as the number of rings on the handbell when announcing visitors: two rings for a man, one for a woman, and one and a half for a priest. From such memories he developed the imaginary palace of Donnafugata, an Arabic derivative meaning "closed fountain", in *The Leopard*. It was a literary congress he attended however, that resolved him to write a novel. *The Leopard* completed, he died in Rome in 1957.

Chapter 8

THE LEOPARD

"The crowd of peasants stood there silent, but their motionless eyes emitted a curiosity that was in no way hostile, for the poor of Donnafugata really did have a certain affection for their tolerant lord who so often forgot to ask for their little rents of kind or money; also, used as they were to seeing the be-whiskered Leopard on the palace facade, on the Church front, above the baroque fountains, on the majolica tiles in their houses, they were glad to set eyes now on the real animal in nankeen trousers, distributing friendly shakes of the paw to all, his features amiably wreathed in feline smiles."

So you have fallen asleep, old friend. It is late, and all the others have left; but for you there is no point in getting home to bed: it is the night of the new moon, and you must catch the propitious moment to go out and gather rosemary on the Pietrazzi rocks – with a brazen sickle, no doubt. Yet this is Sicily in the year of Our Lord 1861, and coming here to my home village from Palermo, from the Prince of Salina's Palace, it is always a shock to find the old superstitions thriving, and the local herbalist still influential and busy. I suppose, as a priest, and a strict Jesuit to boot, I should disapprove of your antiquated spells, your brews and mumbo-jumbo; but I know that when you sell one of your potions to the village women – whether it's for broken hearts or swollen feet – you always tell them it will be useless without an accompaniment of Aves and Glorias. In our different ways, we cooperate in the business of mending humanity...

And now my philosophical abstractions have sent you to sleep, Don Pietrino, I can talk more freely. You see, it's not so simple as a matter of politics, these changes we see around us. All of you here this evening, gathering at my mother's house to welcome me after my years of absence in the Prince's household – all of you were hoping that I, who mingle with the mighty, would bring comforting news to you about the united Italy: this new country that even we proud, independant Sicilians find ourselves caught up in... Yet how often in the past you people have said that Sicily, Italy, the world – and especially the poor of the world – needed things to change. Be truthful, old friend: you yourself used to say so – not just the impatient young hotheads, nor the jackal opportunists, but simple, honest men like you—

No, not me: the Church prefers tradition: a *status quo*, built on rock. Well, as I said this evening, you have your "progress" now, and this is it: this united and godless Italy, with its new taxes, its expropriation laws, even conscription – not exactly the "liberty, security and ease" folk used to go on about! And I remember that crafty steward of the Prince's saying, "Everything will be better: the priests will be the only ones to lose on the deal – God looks after poor folk like

me, not them." This, mark you, over a "missing" bottle of Don Fabrizio's own wine, like as not. Oh, and *he* has done very well for himself since then, thank you – but I doubt if God had much of a hand in it...

Well, as you must have seen, *I* have no confort for you. I do indeed mingle with the mighty in the palaces of the Prince of Salina, and even attend some of his most private interviews – for the family priest is always in attendance, unobtrusively, studying his breviary in a corner of the room. Moreover I have been fortunate in my Prince: he has been a good master to me; and though, in the service of my greater Master it has been my unpleasant duty at times to take him to task, he has always been a loyal protector: you may not know this, but it is only due to him, to Don Fabrizio himself and his talent for moving with the times, that I was exempted from the general expulsion of the Jesuits under the present regime. Call him a collaborator if you will, but he bent with the storm and survived: the new generals became his friends, they saw to his family's safety – and recently they even offered him a place in the new Senate.

He declined this, in fact: gracefully, I am certain. He told me afterwards that he tried to explain his reasons to the Cavalieri, secretary to the Prefecture, who had been despatched to impart the tidings of this great honour – "For so he clearly considered it, Father," he said to me; "and I found myself attempting to describe the Sicilian character to him, something of what has made us the way we are: our climate, our history as a perpetual colony; how we hate change; and how we have learned a passive, hair-splitting, stubborn resistance over two thousand odd years. But how could he understand? – that I was a member of the old order of ruling classes, full of bad habits and empty of illusions... I declined; but I presumed to offer a word of advice to the Prefecture: make Don Calogero Sedàra a Senator, I said: he is just your man."

I knew he had been seriously upset, that day – not just the bitterness and the world-weary look, nor the cynicism of his "advice": when I went to the study later to check some figures for our evening session of star-gazing, I found the cross had been snapped off the top of the alabaster model of St Peters on his desk. He sits there caressing the dome, you see, while he is talking...

He is a complex man, my Prince: the noblest, cleverest, most masterful and most honourable man I have ever known or will ever know – and my greatest

Preceding pages: Donnafugata – "enclosed fountain" – was the Leopard Prince's favourite country retreat. At the height of the Sicilian summer the Salina household made the trek here from Palermo, three days' hard travel in closed carriages.

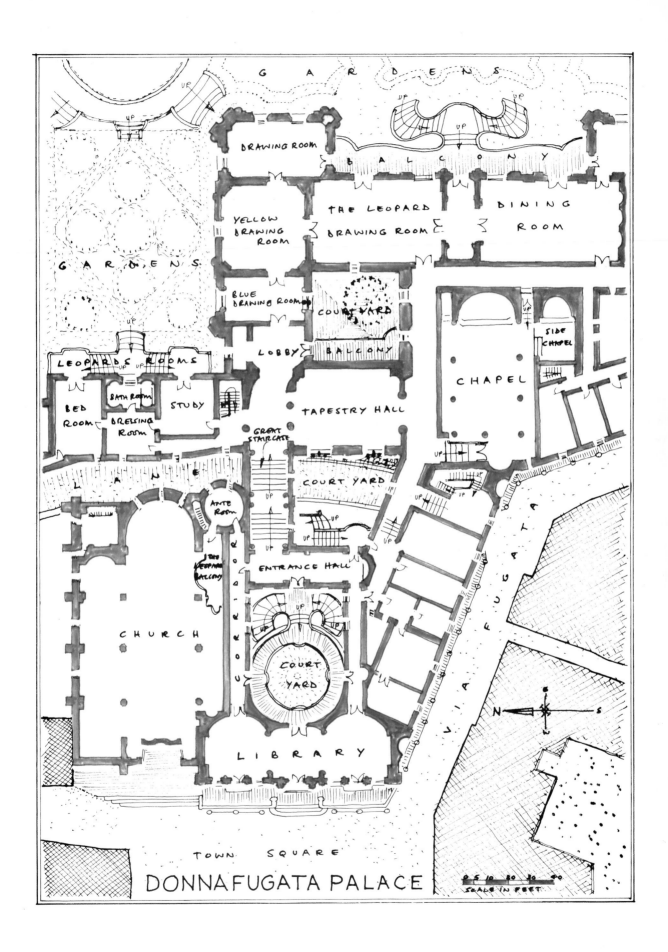

DONNAFUGATA PALACE

friend, without once forgetting his high station. He is also one of the most sensual and worldly of mortals, for which I have repeatedly rebuked him and absolved his confession; and God knows it is the nature of that great fair giant – gigantic in his apetites too – to behave imperiously and be accustomed from birth to the indulgence of his wants as by right. . . But he is also one of the saddest and wisest of men, Don Pietrino: for he saw the changes coming; recognised their inevitability and adapted to them; saw too, with an awful clarity, the diminution of the aristocratic idyll he loved and had always taken for granted. And he was determined, however sharp the humiliation, to drink that bitter draught: to secure the survival of his family and possessions at any cost. And he has succeeded. But oh, what a fall was there!

He was never a businessman, you understand: his great villa on the Salina lands outside Palermo – the most beautiful of his mansions, though not his favourite – his palace in the city, his thousands of rich acres near the coast, and his even vaster tracts of country inland – none of these were ever run for profit. He was not concerned to increase his great wealth or position: a discreet philanthropist, a casual, even a careless landowner, with all the aristocrat's sublime disregard for commerce – he did not wish to be bothered with the details of management as long as he and his family might live in the manner to which they were accustomed.

His one true passion was astronomy (no, I would not dignify his apetite for women or fine food by such terms): he is, you realise, internationally acclaimed, and has been given a medal for his contribution to the science. As for me, I have been privileged to work as his humble colleague in this perusal of the stars; by the grace of God, mathematics, like Latin, is a sort of natural element to me. We spend much of the day in the observatory that crowns the villa; and when he takes his household to his country estate at Donnafugata, one of the smaller telescopes always travels with him.

Donnafugata. *That* is his favourite home: a hard, poor, upland town that has barely altered over a century, built into a fold of the barren, unalterable hills. It lies a weary three-days' journey from Palermo. Don

Left: *One of Donnafugata's numerous reception rooms. Here amid the fading gilt and baroque splendour, beneath the Murano glass chandelier, the Prince held court.*

Above: *A design of parrots decorates the walls of a salon from the Villa Salina, the Prince's town residence near Palermo.*

Fabrizio always sets out in mid-August (the servants and supplies despatched in advance of course), and stays there until mid-November. This involves travelling through the hottest weather of the whole cruel Sicilian year, in carriages closed against the dust. Even so we always arrive white from head to foot on the third afternoon – to be greeted by all the dignitaries of Donnafugata in their finest robes of office, the town band playing the gypsy song from *Traviata*, and most of the inhabitants, either from devotion to their Prince or for lack of anything better to do in siesta time.

Tradition and protocol is rigid. After the formal greetings, we all proceed to the Mother Church in the main square to give thanks; then at last, and then only, can we approach the Palace itself (where the steward and all the staff and huntsmen are waiting in line); and on the steps we are bidden farewell by the official delegation – but we cannot retreat inside until the

107

Princess has issued her customary invitation for dinner to the most important dignitaries: the mayor, the notary and the priest – to which the Prince adds the church organist; his shooting companion: Don Fabrizio's second passion is hunting.

And this summer, my friend, as we were about to escape, gratefully and finally, into the cool Palace, the Prince surprised us all – and I hear that the townsfolk still talk of it – by raising his hand and announcing that "after dinner *all* our friends will be most welcome". I think it was on an impulse, and one that rose out of his instinct for survival: an innovation in changing times. But, meditating upon it later, and in the light of subsequent events, I think that was perhaps the moment at which his prestige started its long decline.

The Palace at Donnafugata is on the main square next door to the Mother Church. Its front with the seven windows and the great door, the flight of steps, gives no conception of its vast extent, for it runs back some three hundred yards, and its rooms and apartments are innumerable – when I first went there I lost my way several times – and many of the upper bedrooms are not only unused but probably unopened year in, year out. Certainly Don Fabrizio himself has never set foot in some of them; he used to claim, with some satisfaction, that "a house of which one knew every room wasn't worth living in"— Yes, old friend: hard for us to comprehend; but then, so is the vastness of the gulf that divides us from these minor gods.

("Gods" in the pagan sense, of course; and with some remarkably odd pagan habits at various times in the past, so I have heard – as certain very private and shut-away chambers of this old place bear witness. How much should one believe in reports of the little cubicles set round a padded pink salon; of the obscene bas-reliefs, mercifully obscured by time; of the whips and strange instruments...? It is not for us to wonder about, my friend. They are safely buried away now, the entrance concealed behind some vast unmoveable cuboard, I am certain. And I would not think aloud of such matters if any soul were awake in this house. It is all in the past: old sins best forgotten...)

The Palace is set around three courtyards, with the

Left: *The number of its apartments was incalculable; many of its upper rooms may have lain unopened and unexplored for years – certainly the Prince himself had never set foot in some of them, claiming that a house of which one knows every room is not worth living in.*

gardens beyond. Its styles are various – there must have been many additions over the years – but in the main a species of Sicilian baroque, I believe, heavily ornate; and this vast establishment is somehow harmonious, and right for the noble line of Salina. Everywhere – and in various parts of the town as well – you may see the rampant leopard in stone or plaster, crumbling and mossy or newly repainted; inside the Palace itself, on coats-of-arms, on cutlery, or carved into the great stone fireplace of the Leopard drawing room, it is always there, like the shadow of past generations.

But there are many drawing rooms, Don Pietrino: the Leopard room, the blue drawing room and the yellow one, the young ladies' own salon, bright with cushions and footstools, embroidery left on a sofa at the ring of the dinner bell... You must walk through many great, unused rooms, shuttered against the sun and the savage midday heat, to reach the tapestried hall and the inside staircase; at the bottom is the door opening onto the outside stairs that lead down into the couryard below – and then, of course, the outer gate and flight of steps into the piazza. There, my friend, you have a simple journey such as one might cover half a dozen times in an ordinary day!

The Prince's own suite of rooms I know well: his study, his dressing-room, his bathroom – the great bedroom I have only seen in passing, with its silk-covered walls and blue-shaded lamps, the Princess's *sal volatile* and other supports (she is given to hysteria) on a table near the bed.

I remember the bathroom particularly clearly: this last visit, August 1860 – (what is it – February, now?) yes: last year, on the very afternoon of our arrival, I needed to speak to Don Fabrizio on an important family matter. He was in his bath; and, thinking – I suppose – it might be some emergency, he had his lackey send me in. Perhaps I was too hasty in my nervousness (I was very anxious about my errand), for he had only just stepped from the tub and stood there mother-naked, streaming – for all the world like the great stone Neptune of the palace fountain. I am accustomed to the baring of souls, but— Well, I averted my eyes and handed him the towel as bidden; and I dried his colossal ankles and feet whilst he attended to the rest. (His blond colouring comes from his mother, you know: the German strain. His father was dark and thick-lipped as any Sicilian; there are miniatures in the study.)

But it was in the Leopard drawing room we waited

Opposite: *The Prince's study where he held his more informal audiences. An avid astronomer, he never travelled without a telescope.*

Left: *Also from the Villa Salina, the Prince's observatory, where he indulged in his passion for astronomy.*

THE OBSERVATORY

that first evening for the guests to arrive. Don Fabrizio always insisted that this occasion should be formal and impressive, with all the trimmings: powdered flunkeys in knee-breeches, punch *alla romana* served before the roast, French wines throughout. But he never wore evening dress, in deference to those of his guests who did not own such things. Imagine, then, the consternation – embarrassment among the adults, giggles from the children – when the new mayor, Don Calogero Sedàra, turned up in tails! Perhaps things *were* changing in Donnafugata. This was an overweening little jackal of a man who had made a great deal of money in the recent and continuing upheavals, and was now – so I gathered – a power to be reckoned with: the New Man, maybe, in a new era.

Then, minutes later, came another dramatic entrance – indeed, another threat, but subtler this time: the daughter of the new mayor, Angelica, whom I could remember as a chit of a girl. Since then the new-rich peasant had sent his jewel all the way to Florence to be polished – and oh, my friend, she was – sensational! She was beautiful, but also quick-witted

and clever at watching and learning. I could see that both the Prince and his favourite, his nephew Tancredi – more precious than any son – were mesmerised by her; caught off their guard by the sheer unexpectedness of this gorgeous apparition, this rare flower rooted in the dusty, desolate square of old Donnafugata, climbing up, so lusty and so fresh, to bloom in their high palace rooms, and scent the very air around her...

And I saw Concetta was upset. It was for her sake that I had bearded her father in his bath: she had confided to me that she loved her cousin Tancredi, and believed he returned the feeling. The Prince had dismissed it as girlish fancy; but, watching her now, I saw how she cared. Saw too that she was being replaced by a peasant girl – in marvellous disguise: a creature whose mother (according to my informants) was not sociably acceptable in Sedàra's new world: just a handsome cow kept at work in the back kitchen – and *her* father had been the village untouchable, a filthy animal whose violent death had to be hushed up. I watched the girl: this gutter-lily, shimmering under the forty-eight-branched Murano chandelier of the

Leopard room; and I confess I shivered, old friend. *She* was progress, *she* was change: here in our midst was the inescapable future.

So you see, even at Donnafugata, things did not stand so still as they seemed to; and that late summer the old Palace witnessed a series of incidents that marked the track of the Salina star descending just as surely as any the Prince and I might watch in the revolving night sky until it slowly dipped below the western hills.

It was from the great library fronting centrally on the square that Don Fabrizio looked through the slats of the shuttered balcony the very next afternoon and saw his beloved Tancredi, in his most elegant clothes, cross the cobbles under the plane trees towards the mayor's house, followed by a lackey with a basket of the best foreign peaches. Signorina Angelica was being courted. And it was to the study that the Prince summoned – no: invited – Don Calogero Sedàra some two months later to ask on behalf of Tancredi for his daughter's hand in marriage. I was there, specifically requested to attend: a helpless, and almost silent, witness; I did not even know what was coming. Indeed, I was thunderstruck; first by the proposal itself – and to see my great golden Leopard forcing a smile, humbling himself, bargaining with and ultimately embracing this jackal – and then (God forgive me for such wordly wonder!) by the catalogue of the bride's dowry: this – this – dungbeetle was counting off *hundred-weights* of gold, *thousands* of acres...!

Now, the Prince knew Tancredi needed to marry wealth: as ambitious as he was penniless, and deeply commited to the new regime – he was away even then, fighting and winning honours on the side of the Garibaldini. His future indeed looked bright, if the money were there. Moreover, Don Fabrizio had dismissed the notion of Tancredi and Concetta with the parting shot: "*She* would not make the ambassador's wife he needs, Don Pirrone, much as I love her: she is too stiff and cool for that." So now he was embracing, and accepting into his family, not only new wealth, but new blood: he embraced a hopeful future – however it might bruise his pride. I was, as I say, aghast; but I could see he was looking to the survival of his line. And in the following months, I think he learned a grudging respect for that terrible little mayor: my Prince recognised an astute mind, and admired the entirely alien opportunism of a cunning entrepreneur. Maybe the jackal too learned something from the Leopard: better table manners? A more graceful way of disagreeing? The address of a good tailor?

But accepting Signorina Angelica to the family bosom was altogether less painful: even the haughty Princess herself forgot her first hysterical reaction to the subject of the marriage under the charm and youthful eagerness of that exquisite creature. The Palace seemed to come alive that autumn, when Tancredi returned from the wars covered in glory, and burning to see his even more glorious betrothed. The corridors reverberated with their laughter as they explored all those long-deserted rooms – and the silences when their chaperone lost them in the maze somehow reverberated even more... All the girls – except Concetta – took Angelica to their hearts; the French governess was thrown into a very ecstasy in anticipation of two such attractive and ardent young people united in love; and I must confess even I found myself moved by the Signorina's proximity to quote a small portion of the Song of Solomon – and cooled myself down over a few Hail Marys in the palace garden. But even there the lusty ilexes, the scent of evening flowers, the fountains themselves, seemed to breathe whispers of earthly love, as Neptune embraced a willing Amphitrite amid the caressing spray rained down upon them by the playful dolphins and tritons all round...

Dear me – I nodded off too, old friend. But I can hear my mother moving about upstairs. Don Pietrino? Are you awake? Yes, you must go about your business. And I will come a little way with you. It's a clear night, and I shall look at the stars while you gather your rosemary.

See, there's Venus low in the West. It is later than I thought.

JEAN RHYS

(1894 – 1979)

Jean Rhys was one of five children born to a Welsh doctor and his Creole wife living on Dominica, one of the Windward Islands. Finding her mother distant and aloof, Jean Rhys became very attached to her father, sharing his fondness for and interest in the native population. From an early age she was aware of the correlation between the real world and that of memory and was fascinated by the scents, moods and colours of the island surrounding her. Night time was "warm, velvety, sweet-smelling. . .but frightening and disturbing if one is alone in the dark".

At her convent school Jean Rhys was inspired to take an interest in literature, but at the age of sixteen she chose to travel to England with an aunt, and after a shaky start at a school in Cambridge, she enrolled at London's Royal Academy of Dramatic Art. The theatre was a welcome change from the grey drabness of England but in 1910 her father died of a heart attack and she had to leave drama school and find employment touring the provinces.

In 1919 she married a Dutch-French writer and left England for Europe. Rhys was happiest in Paris, where she met such contemporary writers as Joyce, Ford Madox Ford and Hemingway, and after divorcing her husband, she lived with Ford and his wife.

In 1934 she returned to England and married Leslie Tilden-Smith. After his death in 1945, she married for the third time and settled in Cornwall. For several years she disappeared from the public eye and her novels went out of print. However, following the dramatisation on radio of her book *Good Morning, Midnight*, she was traced to the West Country where she was at work on her latest novel, *Wide Sargasso Sea*, published in 1966. Interest in her work was rekindled and in 1967 she won the W. H. Smith Literary Award. Jean Rhys died in Exeter, Devon, in May 1979.

Chapter 9

WIDE SARGASSO SEA

"Our garden was large and beautiful as that garden in the Bible – the tree of life grew there. But it had gone wild. The paths were overgrown and a smell of dead flowers mixed with the fresh living smell. Underneath the tree ferns, tall as forest tree ferns, the light was green. Orchids flourished out of reach or for some reason not to be touched. One was snaky looking, another like an octopus with long thin brown tentacles bare of leaves hanging from a twisted root. Twice a year the octopus orchid flowered – then not an inch of tentacle showed. It was a bell-shaped mass of white, mauve, deep purples, wonderful to see. The scent was very sweet and strong. I never went near it.

"All Coulibri Estate had gone wild like the garden, gone to bush. No more slavery – why should anybody *work? This never saddened me. I did not remember the place when it was prosperous."*

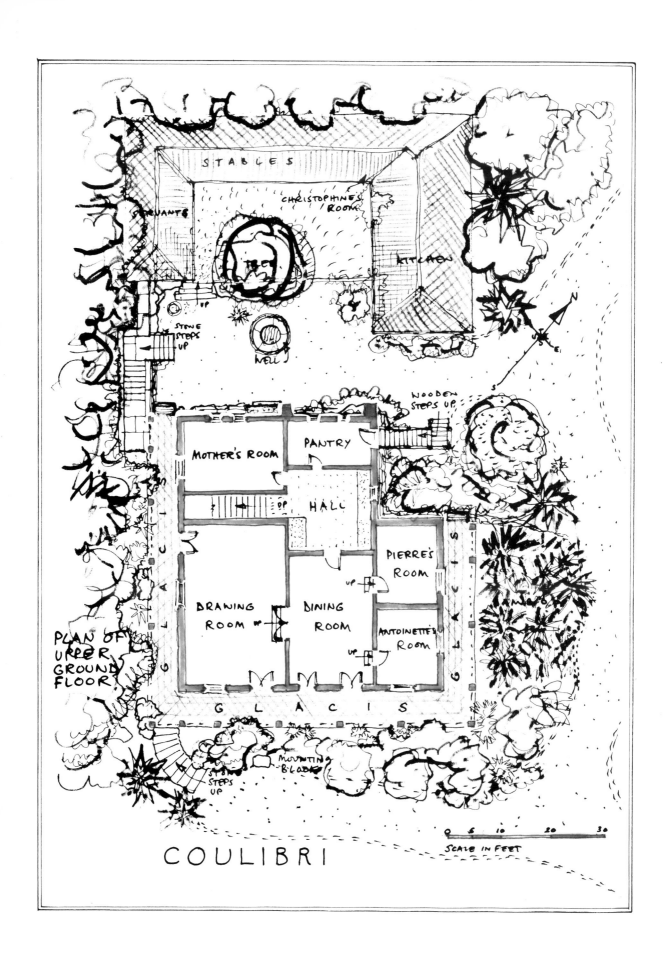

STABLES

CHRISTOPHINE'S ROOM

SERVANTS

KITCHEN

STONE STEPS UP

WELL

N

W E

S

WOODEN STEPS UP

MOTHER'S ROOM

PANTRY

HALL

UP

PIERRE'S ROOM

G L A C I S

DRAWING ROOM

DINING ROOM

ANTOINETTE'S ROOM

UP

S T E P S

PLAN OF UPPER GROUND FLOOR

G L A C I S

STONE STEPS UP

MOUNTING BLOCK

0 5 10 20 30
SCALE IN FEET

COULIBRI

Dearest Sister, As I am still lingering on a small Windward Island, when I should have journeyed to Martinique, I have had no letters for some weeks; and find myself strangely and (*you* will understand this) not unplesantly dissociated from home and the world I know; but look forward to the letters and news that I know are awaiting me in Fort-de-France.

I discover I alloted myself too little time for this excursion into the Windwards; not only is my host – an introduction by way of the Jamaican cousins – a charming man, with a fine house and estate I have had the freedom to explore; but this is an enchanting island, small but spectacular, and I have made a quantity of watercolour sketches to bring home and work up into prints. As I wrote in my last from Martinique, it is a matter of accepting the alien surroundings, and the heat, and giving oneself up to them, along with the slower pace of life; for this is an experience that cannot and should not be "bolted".

But I frequently find myself wondering – probably because already considering how best to describe it to you – what you would think of this wild and wonderful part of the world. You might indeed find it oppressively overgrown and verdant. A riot of vegetation more different from our stark Yorkshire dales is impossible to conceive; and I have been told by my host (an independent bachelor completely taken to the place and the life) of others venturing out from England – younger sons seeking fortunes, or even (am I too fanciful?) rejected suitors "trying to forget" – who have found these tropical rain-forests, and the dearth of equal minds, depressing, and even frightening. I can understand such reactions; and I love Civilisation – yes, and England – too much even to contemplate remaining here. But for the time being – and, as you see, an extension of that time – I am entirely fascinated by it.

I must tell you now that it is not merely landscape that holds me: I have been exploring the forest on horseback and discovering the scattered villages, hamlets, and even some fine old ruined buildings too, that are hidden away in the jungle along narrow paths not even accessible by cart or buggy. In my wanderings I came across an extraordinary old woman with whom I struck up a sort of uneasy friendship (as I will explain) and have revisted several times: to draw her, and meanwhile to "draw" her out about her life and experiences.

You may wonder how a coal-black crone (and not the comely Creole I felt sure you were anticipating!) could charm me so. Take "charm", if you please, more in the Chaucerian sense: forget your society Belle and think instead of Magic... No; let me hasten to assure you, I am under no evil spell; but it is a simple fact, according to all who know her and know of her, that she is a powerful "Obeah" woman and can "see" things to which we ordinary mortals have no access.

But (you say) surely a day's visit to this crone would be enough? True, I sketch swiftly for preference, and – as you often hold – am more accustomed to talk than to listen. But Dora, she told me such a tale – and, something like Sherherezade, keeping her audience each time in suspense, and so with an overpowering need to return for the sequel.

The tale she told me, in a very fragmentary, and often gnomic, form was indeed of that beautiful young Creole maiden of your imaginings; of her parentage, and the house in Jamaica where she grew up; of her marriage to a visiting Englishman – he may have been attracted by her money as well as by her beauty – and their honeymoon on this very island in an old house perched high up among the "pitons" – the abrupt mountain peaks, probably of volcanic origin – above the town of Massacre (now *there* is a name to conjure with; surely worthy of Mrs Radcliffe!) Then of the tragedy that grew out of all this. I hardly dare use the past tense, Dora: much of what I heard I did not understand; yet somehow I received the strong and haunting impression that the tale is unfinished, the *dénouement* still unresolved; and that the final resolution may be such a conflagration of events as to make their past sorrows seem a mere flickering of shadows by comparison. I think it was this sense of continuity, of impending doom, that perhaps held me most strongly; made me return again and again to sit on a box outside her simple hut, as though *this* time I would understand...

The woman's name is Christophine Dubois. She was born in Martinique, and shows that strong French influence: not only talking to her son, and to herself (as she frequently does) in Patois, but spicing her garbled narrative with words whose meaning I could only guess. She had accompanied her mistress

Following pages: *Coulibri, the Cosways' estate near Spanish Town. After the emancipation of slaves, the family lost its money and, untended, the tropical wilderness was taking back its own.*

to Jamaica on the occasion of that lady's marriage to a Mr Cosway, as their housekeeper and, after the husband's death, the family's only servant, it seems, at a house near Spanish Town (not far from the south coast of Jamaica) called "Coulibri". I got the impression that, after the emancipation of the slaves, Mrs Cosway with her two small children fell on hard times, and that the place had gone to rack and ruin.

"But always beautiful, a Garden of Eden – something wild like these same jungle round you, young man," she said, frowning at me. (She has a very black face, with high cheekbones; and there is no knowing how old she may be). "My young *doudou* Antoinette love that jungle-garden. She sit on the moss wall sometimes an hour and hark to the sound of the river... You can see the ocean from the *glacis*" (the verandah) "by the bamboo clump, but never hear it. And she walk amongst the tall fern and ginger-lily and all the flowering creeper that hang down from the tree around – the Tree of Life she call the biggest one – and orchid and all different thing – and crush-flower underneath her foot, smell sweet and rotten: she love even that. But Lord what a lonely child! With only the one small brother not right in him head, and a mother too easy despair and not love her up enough – too young to widow like that and leave to fend for sheself. And black people, black trash from around, they know when White slide down to Poor White, and treat them bad – especially the 'white cockroach' who have many slaves in the past and now no help at all. You know what they do? They even kill off her one horse, her riding horse – can't visit no friend, and no friend come to Coulibri. And she see, as I see, the little daughter turn ragged and sad as a doll, slow but sure; and the mother wasting in the looking-glass, till she know it is all downhill unless she can catch herself a next husband."

Old Christophine told me of the new husband, a rich stepfather for young Antionette and poor little Pierre; and how he refurbished Coulibri. "Black people can *smell* money," said Christophine: "the servants them come back, and the harrassment cease –

or so it seem. But now, only a year after the new marriage, Mistress Cosway wanting to leave Coulibri and go: 'They hate us,' she tell her husband (Mason was his name); 'they hate *you*. And I need some change,' she say. 'Let an agent run this and we will go to Trinidad, or to Antigua' – for he have property there too."

But he laughed at her, the old woman told me: he had poured money into the place, and was not prepared to go on indulging his wife's whims. "I will bring in some 'coolies', my dear, to work on the estate: these blacks are too lazy and foolish." He pointed out it was natural that the people round should not like her or her family after generations of slave-owning; "Yet, during the five years when you were alone here with the children, they never actually harmed you." (Here the crone added darkly: "Them, they never *dare* – while Christophine Dubois watch over her;

Below: The veranda – *or* glacis – *where the few visitors might take their rum in the cool.*

they know I have the Power..."

Sometimes I was puzzled as to which house she was speaking of, and which Mistress; for she would switch from telling how "she" loved to dance on the *glacis*, bending back on "his" arm until her long black hair touched the paving stones, to tales of her *doudou* in a scarlet dress by candlelight, with frangipani in her hair: "more beautiful than the moon self"; and how "that half-breed trash Amélie take her place in him bed – and she only next door must hear and the madness start to creep up on her – I curse that trash-girl – and I curse Daniel Cosway, a wicked yellow man, half-breed again: half-brother, he claim; and write wickedness, all about my *doudou* and her bad blood, to the husband. And those evil words cut off him love so BAM" – she was chopping yams, and brought down the knife with a vicious blow – "Is the finish of that sweet honeymoon. He make her drunk with love, then – no more."

I think her *doudou* is always Antoinette, the daughter; and her English husband a Mr Rochester,

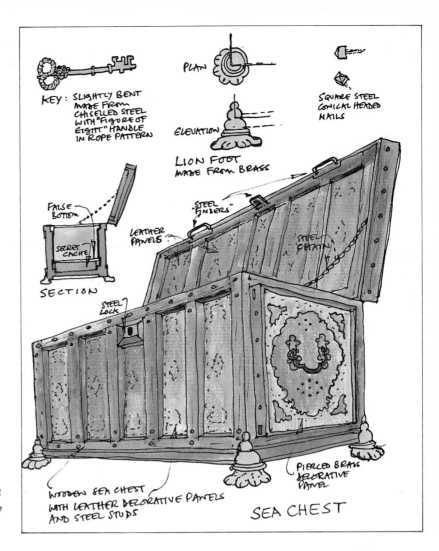

KEY: SLIGHTLY BENT
MADE FROM
CHISELLED STEEL
WITH "FIGURE OF
EIGHT" HANDLE
IN ROPE PATTERN

PLAN

SQUARE STEEL
CONICAL HEADED
NAILS

ELEVATION

LION FOOT
MADE FROM BRASS

FALSE
BOTTOM

STEEL
FINGERS

LEATHER
PANELS

STEEL
CHAIN

SECTION

SECRET
CACHE

STEEL
LOCK

PIERCED BRASS
DECORATIVE
PANEL

WOODEN SEA CHEST
WITH LEATHER DECORATIVE PANELS
AND STEEL STUDS

SEA CHEST

Left: *The dining room, neglected and dusty in the afternoon sun.*

Opposite: *In the corner was an old sea chest, its imposing bulk and brass inlay a symbol of the family's former fortunes.*

who "take her off back to Jamaica and away away to this place 'England' he talk of but I do not believe: I cannot say I Believe since I do not See... But I see my Antoinette – lock up, far from light, from sun, which is her life – where, who know? One small high window I see. Stone walls. And she is cold... And when the gaolor drink deep, sleep sound, then my *doudou* take up the candle – pass through – into dark dark rooms. I see pictures in sewing hang on the wall, and a big bed, and a black clothes-press with the twelve apostle carve there and a dying Christ. Is so I see it. And she pass down the stair and through this great black house like she is spirit – yet fear spirit too: look over her shoulder, and long for light. And she light up all the multitude of candle in the red and white room. And red is the colour of my *doudou* death: flaming red – like the pretty dress that sweet her so..."

"How can you see these things?" I asked, though she had turned away to go into her hut. She did not answer; but neither did she seem to mind when I followed her in. There was an outer room with broken-down chairs; the inner room contained a brass bedstead with a patchwork counterpane. The walls were decorated with pictures of the Holy Family, and "The Prayer for a Happy Death", with a dried-up palm-leaf cross from Palm Sunday tucked behind it. Then I saw a pile of white chicken feathers in the corner of the room. Perhaps that is what she meant to show me, for she said, "There is how I see".

"Is it magic?" I asked. "Is it Obeah? Can you tell me how—?" But she cut me short. "Obeah is not for *béké* like you " – ("white people", I think) – "not for you, young master. Do not enquire into it. *Béké* and Obeah together bring trouble – like when she ask me to make him love her again... For my *doudou* I help how I can. But then only trouble come: worse trouble." And she would not be pressed on this any further. So I complimented her on her brightly-coloured counterpane. She said, "Is what I take from Coulibri, save from the burning... That was the

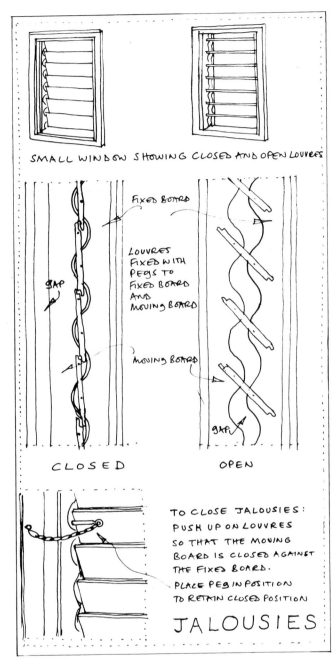

SMALL WINDOW SHOWING CLOSED AND OPEN LOUVRES

FIXED BOARD

LOUVRES FIXED WITH PEGS TO FIXED BOARD AND MOVING BOARD

GAP

MOVING BOARD

MOVING BOARD

GAP

CLOSED   OPEN

TO CLOSE JALOUSIES: PUSH UP ON LOUVRES SO THAT THE MOVING BOARD IS CLOSED AGAINST THE FIXED BOARD. PLACE PEG IN POSITION TO RETAIN CLOSED POSITION

JALOUSIES

Left: *Christophine slept here, devoted maid to Antoinette and her mother before her. The holy picture could barely dispell the feeling that this was the room of a powerful Obeah-woman.*

house she love. And when them trash-folk gather all together – them don't dare, one-one: no sir! but in a pack them brave, brave same way as yellow-dog brave! And them go burn it down. But I cannot speak of that: too much, that terrible night; and too much come of it..."

I returned today, the last day on the Estate, with some small presents for Christophine. I had made a second sketch of her when she was cutting the yams, but she did not care to keep it. "Who want for look at old nigger woman like that? Not me." But she seemd to like the other little watercolour, part of this Jamaican house Coulibri she had so often described to me: the *glacis*, and a black-haired girl in a red dress leaning against the trellised railings. "Is that how it was?" I asked.

"You paint pretty, young man," she said after some long silence: "Is a picture of might-have-been; for my *doudou* never reach to grown lady in that house she love... Is like you mingle-up the two, both mother and daughter, in one person. Is like you see Coulibri never burn-up and she marry with young Sandi, her childhood sweetheart from long back... Maybe you own self, even *béké* like you, can See. And see how mother and daughter each contain that bad seed. But I tell you: is only circumstance, is ill-fortune, bring it to grow and blossom. People say it run in some family, and point to little Pierre who stagger and mumble, never talk. But I say no: is Coulibri ashes hatch out the seed, and the little boy death so soon after – a mercy from God, in truth – come water that seed with bitter tears, and the madness grow and flourish."

"And Antoinette? Did you know the 'seed' was in her too?" I ventured. She shook her head; but she said: "In her sadness I see it; and nurture with loneliness maybe, and fear sheself can go the self-same way she see her mother go – so loose and wild – and how when she lock-up she offer herself to any man she pray might free her." (Was this the mother or the daughter? Did the girl's husband lock her away in the cold room with stone walls and a gaolor because he feared she might—?)

I returned to firmer ground. "But Coulibri," I said, pointing to my sketch: "they were happy there? Before everything went wrong? I mean, for Miss Antoinette it must have been a wonderful childhood: to grow up in a West Indian Garden of Eden... And you say they used to come for holidays to this island, to that very house in the hills above Massacre...?" Then I saw that Christophine – who had turned away from me and held her silence (while I was stumbling on with my questions) – Christophine was weeping, quite silently. So I went close to her (she smelt of spices and clean linen) and put round her wrist my other present: a thin silver bangle to go with the one she wears. Yes, it was a trinket for you, dear Dora; but I shall get you another in Martinique.

Then? Then I whispered farewell and led my horse away from the clearing.

But I am haunted by this girl in the red dress... I confess, that, were I in England now I believe I might be driven – as by some daemon – to follow up what clues I have. Cosway – Mason – Rochester. A handful of names. Shipping lists? The records of Births, Marriages and Deaths in Somerset House? As though If I traced her I could somehow avert the tragedy that seems to hang over her and even over those around her. For I believe now that is what the old woman could see...

But – to come back to solid earth, dear sister! After all, I have my own life to lead, my tour to continue, and my commissions to complete: the St Pierre

church on Martinique, the Government buildings and Cathedral in Spanish Town, Jamaica, and two handsome sugar plantations nearby, if I play my cards right. Maybe when I am in Spanish Town I will seek out what is left of this Coulibri: its high foundations, the stone-flagged *glacis*, the curved flight of steps – these may still remain. And the stone mounting-block. All hidden in the jungle: a wild garden of Eden that has thrown off the dominion of God's order, and of Man's frail reason.

ALAIN-FOURNIER

(1866 – 1914)

Alain-Fournier was the pseudonym of Henri Albain, born and brought up at La Chapelle d'Anguillon, a small village in the Cher region of France. His father was the village schoolmaster and Alan-Fournier was deeply attached to his native province, although this was combined with a desire for exploration and adventure.

At the age of eighteen, he visited an exhibition at the Grand Palais in Paris and it was here that he noticed and followed a petite blonde girl accompanied by an elderly lady. After several days of roaming the Paris streets in search of her, he found the girl and talked with her for some time. She closed the conversation with these words: "What's the good? We're children. We're silly". The two did not meet again until 1913 when she was already married with two children. However, Alan-Fournier could not forget her and she and her words are echoed in the character of Yvonne de Galais in *Le Grand Meaulnes*.

Alain-Fournier trained both as a teacher and a journalist and spent some time writing for the *Paris-Journal*. In 1912 he completed *Le Grandes Meaulnes*, his only novel. He was mobilised at the start of the Great War, to be killed in action in September, 1914.

Chapter 10

LE GRAND MEAULNES

"It must have been getting on for three in the afternoon when at last he saw the spire of a turret above a large grove of fir trees. 'Some forsaken old manor,' he surmised. 'Some deserted pigeon house. . .' But he kept wearily to his course. At a corner of the wood he came upon two white posts marking the entrance to an avenue. He turned into it and had not gone far when he was brought to a halt in surprise and stood there, stirred by an emotion he could not have defined. Then he pushed on with the same dragging steps. His lips were cracked by the wind which at moments almost took his breath away. And yet he was now sustained by an extraordinary sense of well-being, an almost intoxicating serenity, by the certitude that the goal was in sight, that he had nothing but happiness to look forward to."

132

As children we only knew of the de Galais, and Les Sablonnières; but when they decided to fill up that decrepit château with festivities to celebrate young Franz's engagement, all the children of the neighbourhood – some, indeed, from as far away as Paris – were summoned; and we went too.

It was general knowledge that Franz had always been a wayward and fanciful boy; people say he never grew up. But his parents could refuse him nothing; and on this occasion the fancy took him to create the scene of a kind of Fête Champetre – although it was well into December, and those fields blue with morning frost – to welcome home his wife-to-be.

The dilapidated, sparsely-furnished mansion was swept and garnished; servitors, musicians and players were hired, as well as all the necessary fancy-dress costumes, properties and playthings for their young guests. No expense had been spared in providing entertainment – such rumours at least had reached the excited and well-scrubbed ears of the many children who flocked there in carriages and farm carts that late wintry afternoon, with grandparents to watch over the youngest ones.

We had only ever seen the turret of Les Sablonnières at a distance, rising like a deserted dovecot above the fir-wood. Now our crowded cart turned off the lane between white gates and into the trees. The gravel of the drive had been swept in pleasing semicircles, and my grandmother remarked this was truly like a "proper fête" – at which we children grew even more excited, but quietly, hushed by the dark encirclement of the firs.

At a turn in the winding drive, ahead of us in the gloaming, three fantastically dressed little figures ran across; the tallest, a boy, carried a lantern that showed us his dapper uniform and red cloak, and the bobbing plumes and flounces of the two small girls – all swallowed up in an instant by the darkness of the trees on the other side.

The drive led into a courtyard, and we followed the tall Berlin coach ahead of us through this into a sort of

Left: *In every corner was a jumble of treasured objects: fancy-dress, books, candlesticks. Still mystified, Meaulnes donned a rich waistcoat for the fête.*

Preceding pages: *At first sight you could not be sure of the nature of the building – all you could see was a spire above the trees. But as you approached, there was excitement in the air.*

paddock, already nearly filled with every sort of transport from small phaetons to great four-wheeled carriages. The last light was fading and a cold wind blew as we made our way back into the court, beyond which lay the gardens and the château itself.

The outhouses and stables ranged about us seemed hives of activity. Though all the doors were missing, and many of the windows no more than gaping holes, they had been hung with coloured Chinese lanterns that rocked in the wind, and from somewhere far away came the sound of music.

A very grand gentleman of at least fifteen, in glorious evening dress, hailed us and directed us into one of these outhouses where we found hampers of fancy-dress, piles of swords and sashes and hats and precious trinkets, and beds and tables spread with what seemed to us untold riches: candlesticks and goblets and old mandolins, all jumbled togehter in profusion. Children ran to and fro, trying on hats and fancy waistcoats before a great tarnished looking-glass; fixing each others' sashes, or rifling through boxes for pumps to replace their heavy boots and clogs. We were soon as grand and strange as any; and a group of us, with grandmother in charge, set out through the windy darkness towards the distant lights of the château.

If we had been dazzled before, we were now struck dumb with wonder as we entered through the great double doors, and were unwrapped and let loose in that great festive shell of a house. We explored the maze of corridors, the music rooms, ballroom, dining rooms and drawing rooms. Some doors led only into lumber rooms, unswept, stacked with broken furniture and garlanded with cobwebs. Elsewhere, though the chairs and sofas were threadbare – or so my grandmother remarked – they seemed very rich to us. But we gradually lost our awe and joined in with the excited throngs of revellers to watch the mounte-bank entertainers, dance to the music or simply run squealing through the long passages, chased by a gangling pierrot from the troupe of players.

When it was time to eat, the company sat down on benches at trestle tables in a broad, low room like a huge farmhouse kitchen, with a blazing log fire in the hearth. Looking around, I wondered whether Monsieur or Madame de Galais were there, or Mademoiselle Yvonne, the young lady of the house; where was Franz himself, the cause and centre of all these celebrations? And when might we see his bride-to-be? But I tucked into the marvellous spread while I

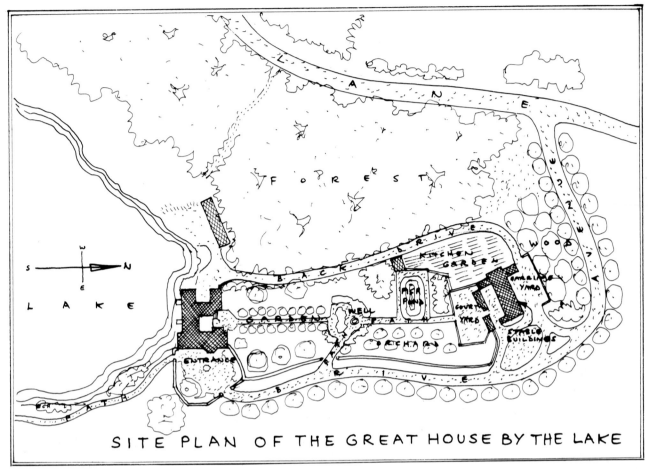

SITE PLAN OF THE GREAT HOUSE BY THE LAKE

Left: The music room. This was a place of tranquility – a refuge from the chatter and bustle of the neighbouring dining room. Here you could sit on the soft, velvet-covered sofa and flick through the worn pages of a picture album.

listened to the older folk gossipping and arguing.

Franz had gone to Bourges, it seemed, to collect the young lady. "And did you hear about how they first met?... Ah, well it seems he fell in love with her at first sight—" "So young to marry! Too young, some say—" "But then, Master Franz always had his own way—" "And that's not all: His own house too— you must know *that*! Oh yes: as a child – and, true enough, he's not much more now – he demanded his very own little house. His father gave him that isolated cottage beyond the wood – and he would go off there alone, and other children would join him and tend his garden and ride his donkey and share in his picnics... Yes indeed: the young bridegroom will have a ready-made home for his bride."

I was tired out with all these wonders and found myself nodding. There was a lantern-show in progress

in the parlour; but I found a room nearby – another dining room I think, where many of the younger children were looking quietly through picture albums while sweet music came from a piano in the apartment beyond. Among the children there was a big lad – seventeen or eighteen as I guessed – half-dozing, like the two infants who had climbed onto his knees. I do not think he was of the household: the fancy waistcoat and shiny pumps were somehow at odds with his broad hands and rough hair; and when he opened his eyes, I remember, he wore that same look of mystified awe that I myself had felt all evening, as though he did not quite believe in his surroundings...

In the morning we saw the château properly for the first time, and explored by early sunlight the gardens and paths and courtyards we had stumbled through the evening before. We discovered the round pond and the well, the long, arched pergola of roses run to brambles, and ancient espalier fruit-trees leaning out from crumbling walls. Now we could see what we only knew from gossip: that Les Sablonnières was indeed in a ramshackle state; the mansion itself badly in need of repair: "He really ought to marry an heiress, that

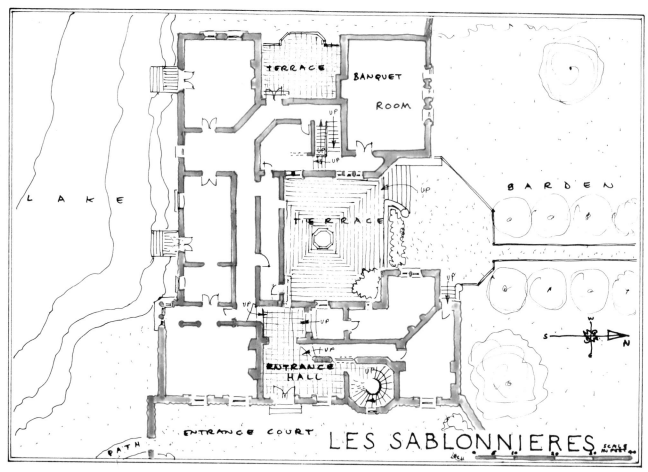

young Franz, if he's to save a great warren of a place like this." But it was a childrens' paradise. We clambered over the ruined walls, played at hide-and-seek through the wilderness of the once-formal shrubbery, as unconcerned as a flock of hedge-sparrows for the future of this spacious domain that was ours, magically, for a night and a day.

Venturing round the length of the great end wing, we found that one side of the château stood on the very edge of a broad, reedy lake. There were boats, moreover, waiting at a landing stage, and the revellers were gathering for an excursion. Again I saw the tall youth. He was talking to a beautiful young lady, very plainly dressed. Grandmother pointed her out as Mademoiselle de Galais; and said we were going for a picnic to the house of the young lady's brother.

"Ma'mselle Yvonne must be worrying about him," she went on; "he may not be home with his fiancée before three in this afternoon, so people are saying – but really! We're all beginning to wonder..."

We did not wonder except at the marvels of such an adventure: the boat-trip, then landing and racing along winding paths through the spinneys and out

Opposite: *From this side, Les Sablonnieres seemed a different building. A courtyard with a well in the middle led to a series of outbuildings, some with broken windows and doors hanging from their hinges. Once a splendid château, it was beginning to crumble and decay.*

Over page: *There was a light on the farmhouse – all that was left of Les Sablonnières. It became the young couple's first home and there, later, she waited for Meaulnes to return from his hopeless quest.*

into the open meadow, where the company converged on a dear little house, all by itself in the wild. No one lived there, it seemed, but it was quickly filled with festive invaders busy devouring the cold lunch that had been brought up from the boats. Fortunately it was a mild day; there was still frost in the shade, and crackling ice at the edge of the water, but the sun was bright and warm; and when we got back to the château in the afternoon, pony races were organised on the sloping meadow behind the home farm...

That farm, with the house attached to it, is all that remains of the enchanted domain. For a few seasons

the mouldering turret of the chateau was still visible above the wood, and a boy I knew who ventured in there hunting had come across uninhabited ruins among the trees, choked with invading scrub and flowering weeds. Then the château and grounds were sold, and the remaining walls razed to the ground by the new owners to enlarge their coverts for shooting.

Looking back now, one might almost see the point of no return for Les Sablonnières was the moment on that chill and golden afternoon when the motley crowd of young and old, gathered there for Franz's whimsical fête, began to feel something had gone wrong. No one knew what, but the rumour spread through the old people and quickly cast a shadow over the childrens' play. Suddenly everyone was packing up and leaving; the travelling players were the first to vanish, decamping swiftly like gypsies, while the musicians were still muttering about payment. Infants were hurriedly divested of their borrowed splendour. I well remember wishing I could take home the little jewelled sword I had been wearing at my belt – yet somehow I knew it was part of the dream and, like faerie gold might turn to dust and cobwebs outside the enchanted boundaries of the Domain.

There were no coloured lanterns that evening, and it was dark when we joined the throng in the carriage park. Till then, it had all been undertones and hissed orders to make haste; but now there was the racket of a retreating army, shouts to "back up there!", shrill cries of "Wait for me!" – the crunch of wheels and the whinny of startled horses. It was cold in the cart queuing to move out and down the drive. I was nearly asleep, curled up beside my grandmother. But I have a recollection – or maybe I dreamed – of the gangling pierrot loping by and stopping when she called to him. "They found a note," he said, "telling how the young lady had deserted him... Yes, and now they're saying he must have come and gone away again: they fear for his life – he may be desperate... I must find him – must find him – so young and fond and foolish—"

It was years later that I heard the whole tale: how Franz's disappearance had led, through the debts of past follies, to the dissolution of the Domain. And at last I began to see how Franz, his fugitive bride, his beautiful sister, and that same tall lad, my secret hero, were all linked by childhood vows – a sort of mad and loyal chivalry – in an endless search for that enchanted moment of lost youth.

AFTERWORD

Following in the footsteps of LITERARY HOUSES, MORE LITERARY HOUSES creates a series of real houses based on an author's idea, but transforms them from the two-dimensional page through words and pictures into a three-dimensional image. Such a project is, perhaps, foolhardy in the extreme, but endlessly fascinating, frustrating and ultimately rewarding.

For some authors, the house is an all-encompassing literary device—instead of being simply a back drop, it possesses the characters inhabiting it and dominates the book. It can alter to suit the author's wishes—the house may play an important role in the story, but a plot is the deciding factor. Rooms may disappear, shrubberies may be replaced with summer houses and doors may be relocated mysteriously overnight. Or the house may simply be atmosphere, seducing characters and readers alike by its very intangibility. In BUDDENBROOKS, for example, the location of the family home, its occupants, the layout and contents of its rooms, its pictures and ornaments are precisely described, whereas in LE GRAND MEAULNES, the reader is granted only a tantalizing, half-remembered glimpse of a distant turret, echoes of laughter in empty corridors.

As before, the first stage of the project was to decide exactly which books to do. Once the list had been drawn up, the real research began. Each book was read through closely, at least twice, and every reference to period, architecture, structure, furniture and fabric was noted, everything from in which room the family sat to catch the morning sunlight to the particular chipped, green and gold Meissen cup from which the Master took his afternoon tea. Artists were chosen, whose individual style would best complement each particular book and the rooms and points of interest for illustration were selected. Each artist was briefed individually and sent annotated passages from the text, a sheaf of notes, rough ground plans, photographs of nineteenth-century drawing rooms, gardens and the like, all relentlessly gleaned from the clues in the text.

Artists' roughs received, the author mapped a narrative key to unlock the doors of each of the houses, while the architect worked on additional sketches and painstakingly recreated the various sets of ground plans.

At every point, the illustrations were checked against the original book and with the author, designer and editor. The illustrations were also checked against the archival records housed in various museums and libraries for particular references or to follow up a specific requests from the artists for the elusive inkstand, telescope or miniature.

Finally, the text was written to complement the illustrations, drawings and plans, all components coming together to create bricks and mortar from words, to make fiction reality.

ACKNOWLEDGEMENTS

To Alexander R. James, Literary Executor, for permission to reprint from THE PORTRAIT OF A LADY by Henry James; Penguin Books Ltd for permission to quote from Leo Tolstoy; WAR AND PEACE 1, trans. Rosemary Edmonds (Penguin Classics 1957) p.494, copyright © Rosemary Edmonds 1957, reprinted by permission of Penguin Books Ltd; Simon & Schuster for permission to reprint from SUNSET AT BLANDINGS by P. G. Wodehouse; Alfred A. Knopf, Inc. for permission to reprint from the THE CASTLE by Franz Kafka, translated by Edwin and Willa Muir, © 1930 by Willa and Edwin Muir, and BUDDENBROOKS by Thomas Mann, translated by H. T. Lowe-Porter, © 1924 by Alfred A. Knopf, Inc., renewed copyright 1952 by Alfred A. Knopf, Inc.; Pantheon Books, a Division of Random House, Inc. for permission to reprint from THE LEOPARD by Giuseppe di Lampedusa, translated by Archibald Colquhoun, © in the English Language translation William Collins Sons & Co. Ltd, London and Pantheon Books Inc., New York, NY, 1961; the Wallace and Sheil Agency for permission to reprint from WIDE SARGASSO SEA by Jean Rhys; and to Oxford University Press for permission to quote from Alain-Fournier, LE GRAND MEAULNES, translated by Frank Davison, © Oxford University Press 1959, reprinted by permission of Oxford University Press.